THE BEST CHRISTMAS EVER

with MARY ENGELBREIT

Illustrated by
MARY ENGELBREIT

Photography by Styling by
JOHN GOULD BESSLER **HEIDI ADAMS**

**Andrews McMeel
Publishing**

Kansas City

The Best Christmas Ever with Mary Engelbreit

©2003 by Mary Engelbreit Ink

Published simultaneously by
Andrews McMeel Publishing and Oxmoor House, Inc.

www.maryengelbreit.com

and Mary Engelbreit are registered trademarks
of Mary Engelbreit Enterprises, Inc.

Library of Congress Cataloging-in-Publication Data
Engelbreit, Mary.
    The best Christmas ever with Mary Engelbreit /
illustrated by Mary Engelbreit.
    p. cm.
ISBN 0-7407-3908-5
    1. Christmas decorations. 2. Christmas cookery.
    3. Handicraft. I. Title.

TT900.C4E516 2003
745.594'12--dc21

                                    2003049777

03 04 05 06 07 MND 10 9 8 7 6 5 4 3 2 1

**Produced by Smallwood & Stewart, Inc.,
New York City
Design: Curtis Potter
Text: Ella Stewart
Recipes: Sarah Zwiebach & Beth Frischberg**

ATTENTION: SCHOOLS AND BUSINESSES
Andrews McMeel books are available at quantity discounts
with bulk purchase for educational, business, or sales
promotional use. For information, please write to:
Special Sales Department, Andrews McMeel Publishing,
4520 Main Street, Kansas City, Missouri 64111.

Good, better, best...

Indeed, holidays can get grades. If we haven't experienced a so-so celebration, how can we rejoice in the Best Christmas Ever? That's the force behind this book, the coming together of all the elements of an exhilarating and deeply satisfying holiday. Every note of the holiday resonates with warmth and good cheer, from the cozy familiarity of feasting with close friends to a new take on Santa's sleigh. And the presents! We'll help you to open your heart and give unto others the most fabulous gifts. That's why this holiday is crowned The Best Christmas Ever.

Mary

It's Time for Mistletoe and Holly

Preview the decorating,
the presents, and all the
delicious festivities you're
about to create!

he holidays are back! Everybody knows the days leading to December 25th are the most exciting of the year. The earliest whispers are heard in November, when the Thanksgiving celebration formally introduces Christmas. Jingle bells sound as familiar as birds chirping; our internal calendars prompt us to start those lists—lists that will in just weeks become the very elements

that bring the holiday home. Take a deep breath and imagine the Christmas of your dreams. Go back to your childhood; do you remember the utter thrill of the holiday. . . the excitement that you could barely contain? The sheer joy?

You can re-create this spirit of wonder now, in your home, in your gifts, and in your hospitality. Rather than yielding to a tide of Christmas demands, step outside, beyond the chaos. You want the comfort and joy Christmas is meant to be about; let these emotions guide you through the season. The story of your family's holiday journey is one you can write and direct yourself. Give the real spirit of Christmas. Make this **The Best Christmas Ever!**

SAVOR THE SIMPLEST JOYS

Previous page and opposite: All the innocence and wonder of Christmas are contained in two simple images. In the crystal cold of December, birdseed ornaments delight little creatures, who in turn enchant us. Make them by mixing birdseed with peanut butter. Press the mix into cookie cutters and allow them to dry. More little creatures, these in the form of figurines shaped by talented hands many Christmases ago, return each winter.

The Art of the Cheery "Hello!"

Whether it's on a bungalow or a castle, your front door deserves to look every bit as fabulous as your tree. It's the front door that extends your welcome to guests and cues them to expect a celebration inside that's rich with warmth and cheer. The first step to creating such a greeting is actually to take a giant step backward. Before a snip of holly is added, look at the door itself. How about a fresh coat of snappy red paint for Christmas? You could play up the drama of the entrance with a thin glaze of gold or silver, or daub on a theatrical snowy trompe l'oeil finish as a stage for your ornaments and decorations. It's all about setting a mood.

CALL ME A SQUARE

Round wreaths are certainly popular, but square wreaths are sadly underrated. If you think about it, a square or rectangular shape lends itself just as well to this kind of outdoor decoration. To make a diamond shape, flip the wreath and hang it by one corner. More dramatic embellishments are appropriate for the wreath's stronger graphic shape. Voilà! You've turned your entry into an original, inviting greeting. WORKSHOP **PAGE 118**

A CHRISTMAS GLOW

Years ago, one of the most beloved outdoor decorations was created with a stencil and Glass Wax, a window cleaner that dried to a snowy white finish. How economical and simple and charming! What's more, there was no dreaded dismantling after the holiday. With a soft cotton cloth, the stencil designs were wiped off to reveal a freshly cleaned window. This trio of stencils is smartened up with variegated holly and chirpy gingham bows. WORKSHOP **PAGE 118**

STAND STILL FOR A STENCIL

Window stencils are pretty close to being the perfect decoration: the designs have a simple sweetness; they are easy to make, and the stencils themselves can be used over and over again. What's more, stencils are applied on the cozy inside of the window, so you don't have to do that frosty foot-stomping dance to keep warm during outdoor decorating. For extra romance, nothing beats vintage stencils—and we modeled ours on that older look, to reflect a simplicity and shimmering beauty of years gone by. Don't feel limited to standard Christmas designs. Choose stencils of bluebirds and Scotties and cherries and berries. A geometric checkerboard, musical notes, and a design of random polka dots will convey the spirit of the season. For the arrival of extra-special visitors, organize a stencil design with an extra-special message: how excited would a little one be to arrive for the holidays and see his name spelled out on your windows?

WORKSHOP **PAGE 119**

Take Inspiration

Is there a symbol your family loves at the holidays?

A prancing reindeer, a glittering snowglobe, a tipsy snowman? Consider delicate but so-resilient birds, contrasted against the harsh winter; they exemplify the triumph of hope over adversity. Draw their spirit through your home. The birdseed ornaments that spin on bare branches outdoors inspired the birdhouse village we created inside, as well as some glass ornaments that will hang throughout the house.

Finally, in a bedroom upstairs, a handful of fragile feathery angels nests within the branches of a white tabletop tree.

WELCOME TO BIRDLAND USA

Why have just one birdhouse when you can live with a cozy village? Poke through your boxes of seasonal decorations or head to the crafts store for a selection of cardboard or papier-mâché birdhouses. There's no need to look for architectural harmony; in fact, the more bizarre the selection the better. Get out the paints and call in the gang. Once the paint has dried, dress the houses up in their Christmas best with teeny wreaths, stockings, and some lucky birds. To create a vertical village, tack vintage cards to the walls of a small bookshelf unit. Set low-wattage lamps at the backs of the shelves and place the houses in position. Complete the arrangement with a few bottlebrush trees, a snowman or two, and a frame of fat red ribbon.

WORKSHOP **PAGE 120**

Christmas with Mary

Come in, come in to Christmas

in the heart of America. Think of it as the North Pole if Mary Engelbreit lived there. In Mary's house the holiday is everywhere, in gestures simple and gestures sweeping, too many holiday trees to count, and special surprises just around each corner. Out of storage come hundreds of fairy lights, wisps of angel hair, treetop stars and every kind of ornament imaginable. In the calm of the dining room, a leggy tree is nearly lost beneath its finery: gold garlands, crystal bells, cupcakes and ice cream cones, toy puppets and toy horses, stars and Santas, baby dolls and mysterious boxes. Does everything match? Of course not! This is a loopy tree that stands tall with delicious treats (after all, it is in the dining room) and precious fragile ornaments (this room is out of reach of the house's bustle). At its top sits a colossal gold star splendid enough for Rockefeller Center.

Christmas with **Mary**

A LITTLE CHILD SHALL LEAD...

Can anyone be too young for Christmas? Even if it's possible, it's certainly not a role for Mary's granddaughter, Mikayla. Just as Mary began her love affair with the holiday and its glorious decorations when she was a wee girl, Mikayla has found Christmas a terrific way to express her own decorating glee. An exuberant, original painting on brown paper provides the arresting background for a simple Santa in an outrageous cast-iron peacock sleigh. For extra realism, a pair of snowy evergreens arrive.

ACCESSORIZE, ACCESSORIZE

There's so much telling in the details. A bare tree is the little black dress of the holiday, just begging to be smartly accessorized for the festivities. The branches of Mary's lanky table tree invite all manner of hanging items. This is the tree that will feature some of Mary's most delicate, precious ornaments (including a gold pocket watch). Shapely garlands of gold balls and gold stars provide the vertical links from branch to branch. Given all its golden glamour, Mary finishes the tree with a quirky puppet and strands of crinkled vintage five-and-dime tinsel.

kids
can do it!

Remember Me

Coming up with good gifts for my colleagues at the Engelbreit Studios is a challenge. One year, I created a handmade journal for each artist. They were thrilled at a gift so personal and meaningful to us all, since we share this great passion for paper and pencil.

Mary

The better part of one's life consists of one's friendships.

~Abraham Lincoln~

Christmas Will Come, One Day at a Time

Make the waiting fun! A modest paper Advent calendar with tiny chocolates behind its shutters was the inspiration for this magnificent heritage fabric wall quilt. Crafted of cotton and batting, the piece includes all kinds of prints and patterns, and it's fronted with twenty-five pockets.

Make the sewing fun! We give you the directions, but think of them as a starting point. Like a crazy quilt, your Advent wall quilt can have pieces in varying sizes, and pockets in the shapes of circles and triangles and kidney beans. Position the pockets horizontally rather than vertically. Or let the pockets be scattered about as if they were planets in the solar system.

Dear Friend

Part of my passion for all things Christmas is seeing my holiday stuff again every December. I suppose I do have more than most folks, so the reunion each winter keeps me in the holiday spirit for a full year. And there are always a few pieces out in my house whatever the month.

Yours, Mary

This is the project for all those remnants and scraps that accumulate through the year.

Mix holiday prints with bits and pieces of outgrown clothes, worn tablecloths and napkins, even bed linens. Tie the look together with simple, consistent numerals that indicate Advent dates.

How about a wall quilt for the school — or Sunday school — with each child's initials instead of dates. Smaller versions are outstanding when they're filled with art materials. A bathroom Advent wall quilt is perfect for surprise toiletries or toothbrushes if you have a really big family, or when you're expecting a lot of Christmas company.

25 Ways to Make the Waiting Easier

1 A baby doll and a storybook

2 Christmas socks

3 A penny and a tiny horn

4 Christmas mittens and a toy train

5 A sketchbook and pencils

6 Santa sleep cap and lucky coin

7 A snowman with a peppermint cap

8 Candycanes and a watercolor set

9 Peppermint sticks and lucky charms

10 A snowman jump rope

11 A clay lollipop and wooden puppet

12 A really good photo in a frame

13 Some vintage children's books

14 One tiny antique toy truck

15 A handheld mirror

16 A disposable camera

17 Calligraphic pen, india ink, fancy paper

18 Blocks for the season

19 New Year's resolution guideline list

20 Miniature pine garland wreath

21 All sorts of candy

22 Treasure map to hidden presents

23 Christmas crackers

24 A spinning top

25 A little engine that will

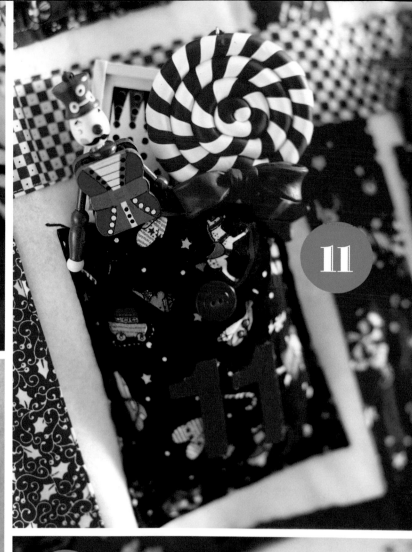

I'M DREAMING OF A
GOOD JUNK DRAWER

Here's how to make your own one-of-a-kind findings garland: spell out the letters of Christmas on office-supply paper tags, then fill the rest of the garland with just about anything you can find in your junk drawer. Strong, heavy cotton cord attaches buttons, bits of ribbon, random pieces of board games gone missing, Scrabble tiles, dominoes, dice, mah jongg tiles, checkers—whatever! This garland is mounted on a length of metal garden chain, so store it hung horizontally to keep it from tangling.

A Holiday Cookie Bazaar

Share Time, Talent & Treats: It's Really Christmas

We've taken the idea behind the quilting bee and given sharing talent a delicious new spin. The result? A Holiday Cookie Bazaar! A party held just so that the lucky guests can share sugary baked goods will produce more celebratory spirit than almost any other social function. The holiday cookie-exchange party has been based on the principle that you can't beat everyone's best. Think about it: each guest brings her specialty cookie, lots and lots of them. Though some people might just assume that all the cookies are wonderful, we recommend, in the interest of

cookie quality control, that each guest should step up to the plate and give every offering a thorough taste test. Complete the menu with pitchers of cold water and mugs of steamy, creamy cinnamon mochaccino capped with a plop of marshmallow cream. Providing mochaccino helps guests cleanse their palates between cookie varieties.

Encourage your bakers to bring along recipe cards so their delicious specialties can be re-created (and checked for food allergies if necessary). A local baking-supply store or an on-line bakery source will have sturdy cardstock boxes, fluted paper cups, and a cone of cotton kitchen string. You'll want to have lots of colorful tissue paper around to protect the cookies as they are packed up for their journeys to happy homes across the neighborhood. One item you can forget: a "No Sampling!" sign!

TOP THE TABLE

Plan to display cookies so that everyone gets a good look. Give a flourish to specialties like sparkler cookies (opposite). A versatile sugar cookie dough is shaped into our sparklers, which were baked after they were pressed onto paper lollipop sticks. The decorated cookies nestle in rock-candy snow in tin pails covered with vintage cards. Paper lace doilies (above) unify mismatched china; it all looks so Christmasy! ▓ PANTRY **PAGE 103**

It's here to share joy and cheer; this is the beauty of a **cookie!**

FINISHING THE COOKIES

Even brawny bar cookies are delicate, so have a beauty repair station ready as guests arrive. Patch broken cookies with melted chocolate or marmalade. Liberally sift confectioners' sugar over any breaks or bruises. Sprinkle colored sugars, dragées, cocoa, or chocolate shavings on cookies. What is the ultimate fixer? Try royal icing (a mix of confectioners' sugar and milk) spooned into pastry bags and piped on cookies for coverage or to hold small decorative candies in place.

PANTRY **PAGE 100**

Just Add Love
Holiday

We found the perfect container for the precious cookie cargo: vintage ornament boxes. Some even have divider inserts that will hold stacks of cookies. Once a box is filled, tie it securely with string or ribbon and consider it fragile. Carry these with all the care you'd give a wedding cake.

Copy
our tote
exactly

Turn to page 140 for
the Mary Engelbreit
artwork

LET IT SNOW!

Carry Christmas in Your Heart & on Your Shoulder

"Where did I put the packing tape?" "Where is that gift list?" "What am I looking for?" Far too much time in busy December is spent looking for things — wrapping paper, crafts materials, decorations, swatches and samples — and lists, lists, lists. Set yourself up to avoid this pointless hunting with a catch-all holiday tote.

"I wish I had remembered that!" "Did I give her the same book last year?" "How many Christmas cards did we end up sending out?" Jot down these key bits of information in a notebook or whatever paper is handy. Put everything together in a file you can retrieve next November.

MEMORIES ARE MADE OF THIS

While memories are still fresh, scribble down notes you'll find helpful in another eleven months. A custom folder held together with bright ribbon will keep your jottings, updated addresses, and important details in one handy package. Just think, next year you'll know immediately how tall last year's tree was, how many strings of lights you needed, who is not fond of Brussels sprouts, and how to reach Cousin Howard to find out how many extra guests he'll be bringing.

IT'S IN THE BAG

We chose an impossible-to-overlook scarlet canvas bag that is roomy and tough enough to hold all kinds of stuff. Then we customized the tote with fringe, trim, and an iron-on transfer, so it can be spotted in a second. Because it's so distinctive, it acts as a reminder just in itself. We plan to call this tote into service every December for a long, long time to come.

WORKSHOP PAGE 124

The Stockings Are Hung

Now's the time to play
and make good cheer;
Santa's visit is quite near.

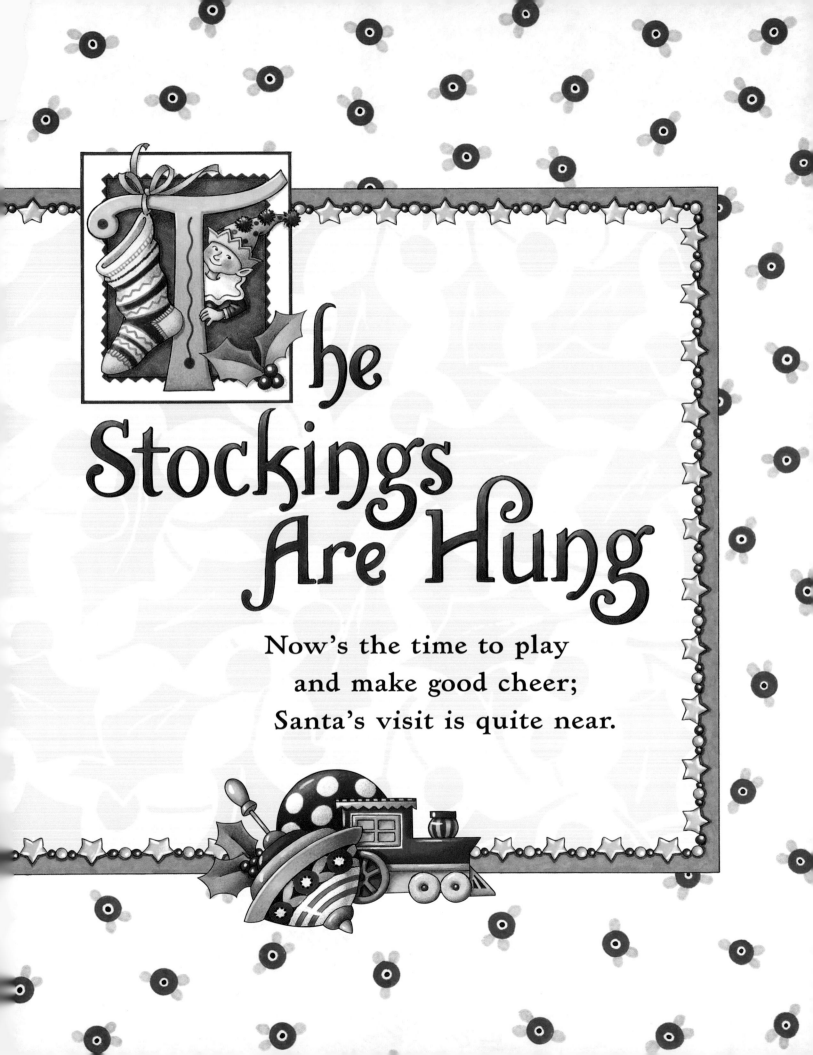

lease join us! When asked what they wish for the holiday, most everyone responded "more time with friends and family." We're here to tell you how easy that can be. Not to mention more gratifying than trudging through the local malls, vacuuming the pine needles from the carpet, practice-testing a complicated new dessert for Christmas Day callers. The secret? Forget the mall,

the vacuum, the tortuous dessert. You hereby have

our permission—indeed our encouragement and our

blessing—to fill your holiday

with friends and family to your

heart's content. They'll love it,

you'll love it, and your wish will

finally have come true.

To accomplish this attainable ideal, you'll likely

need to set some new priorities. Say you're faced with

scheduling thirty hours of activities into a single day.

For The Best Christmas Ever, delegate, deploy, and

dismiss as never before. Put your holiday energy into

what you truly love, be it decorating or baking; cut

and slash your way through obligations, the lists of

chores, and whatever you don't want to do. That's it!

Calling All Decorations, Calling All Lights

Front and center! It's time to round up the elements that are about to transform your home.

Most families decide where to place the decorations through some debate; compromise is in the spirit of the holiday, except for those few absolute, hot-button issues (how tinsel is placed on the tree is a good example). Whatever your tradition, if it's to poise each piece in its own special place, to try something new every year, or to go somewhere in-between, the process is above all a golden opportunity to savor the renewal of the Christmas season.

HOLIDAYS WRAPPED IN LOVE

Do you fall in love with your decorations all over again each December, only to store them the rest of the year in a bunch of tattered cardboard cartons or plastic boxes? Storage can be beautiful. Toile-covered boxes smartly tied with ribbons keep ornaments safe on shelves or dressers in any room of the house. And each time you see the boxes, you'll smile knowing the treasures they hold. WORKSHOP **PAGE 124**

WHEN ORNAMENTS BECOME ART

Many of us have come to cherish the exquisite but fragile ornaments of earlier generations. Each year the dilemma is whether to keep the baubles safely stored or hang them on the tree and nervously hope not to hear the tinkle of delicate glass hitting the floor. Our solution: display these treasures prominently but as safely as if they were in a jeweler's case. This shadowbox is made with new materials but has a properly vintage look, and it's deep enough to accommodate the dimensions of the prizes within. Secure the ornaments in position with removable adhesive and finish the look with a drape of silver beads.

Take Inspiration

One fabulous piece can set the decorating tone for an entire event.

If you've got a room to decorate for a holiday party, supper,  or a casual get-together with friends, check out your vintage greeting cards for a design that reflects the spirit of the event. If you're looking to bring cheer to a guest room, the kitchen, even the powder room, look again to vintage cards. The copyshop can print out the artwork to just the size you want. One request: we have a real empathy for the hard-working illustrators of cards, so please do not reproduce artwork except for use in your home, and never for sale!

WORKSHOP PAGE 125

A CUT & PASTE CHRISTMAS

People have tried everything, it seems, from stringing clothesline across the living room to bending wire hangers into mobiles, to keep good greeting cards on view for the season. A nifty solution? Choose from a bunch of vintage and new cards and mount them on scraps of wrapping paper. Frame them in glass, and embellish the glass with rickrack, ribbons, peppermints, jingle bells, and tinsel rope. The cards are hung in groups from giant pushpins, so the display will grow along with your mementos of each year. What an intriguing, inviting decoration this makes, and because the cards are slipped behind glass, it eliminates the awkward situation of revealing personal messages written inside the cards. This is the kind of versatile decoration that can be made with whatever's on hand. Be careful, though; once you get into the spirit of putting all the pieces together, you may find it hard to stop!

WORKSHOP PAGE 126

A Friends Christmas Feast

Share Memories, Pass around Laughter & Serve Fabulous Foods

We must get together over the holidays!" Talk about easier said than done. Entertaining at the holidays, for all the good intentions, is often more daunting than at any other time of the year. The invitations, the menu, the decorations—yes, they will take over your life if you let them. This year, deliberately adopt a looser attitude and marvel at the difference. You know your guests will relish the chance to spend time together; the question, then, is "How can I make this easy?"

We've created a feast, a colorful, yummy, leisurely meal that you can toss together pretty

simply. Let the oven do the work; it will produce a savory-stuffed crown roast pork, baked squash, and a fabulous sugary fruit focaccia. Oh, the glorious kitchen aromas that will greet your lucky guests.

By virtue of one giant sign, you'll pretty much have taken care of the decoration in a single masterstroke. Then mix up some cocktails and pull together the evening's music. Ask the kids to help pitch in arranging candles, and serve dinner family-style from the sideboard. The combination of great food and the casual environment you create will have guests glowing with satisfaction. This is an event so stylish, simple, and succulent that you may find yourself planning one or two more before the new year is rung in.

A CROWNING GLORY, ALL RIGHT

Roasted squash, focaccia rich with moist, tender fruit, deep green spinach: all are simple foods that share the spotlight with a royal crown roast of pork (above). **PANTRY PAGE 107** In the dining room, the foods are set out to let guests help themselves, a way to loosen up the conversation and at the same time, make the hosting duties that much lighter. **WORKSHOP PAGE 125**

Just Add Love
Holiday
Have you ever seen dreary polka dots? No one has; it is a law that polka dots can only be cheerful and gay. At Christmas, they enliven anything they touch. Keep rolls of ribbon and paper handy and give instant holiday to a doorknob or a photo. There you go! **WORKSHOP PAGE 128**

Three Generations

Wishing you
A JOYFUL CHRISTMAS
and every
HAPPINESS
in the
NEW YEAR

ROCKIN' AROUND
THE CHRISTMAS TREE!

Technology can be a wonderful thing, especially if someone else can do it for you. Enlist the younger generation to compile a CD of favorite music for the holidays, and personalize or create a handmade liner note for the case. To design the label and booklet in the jewel case, pull together a handful of elements that say Christmas to you. Scan the message from an old greeting card, one or two family photos, and patterns and designs on seasonal papers.

■ WORKSHOP **PAGE 127**

Christmas
with Mary

A winter wonderland, of fairies

and snow creatures, heavenly Santas and ethereal angels,
occupies Mary Engelbreit's living room this December. At
the center of the fantasy, a plucky tabletop tree holds court
from a piece of cream-color pottery. And upon that plucky
tree in its pottery throne are lavished crown jewels,
cut-crystal globes, feathered snowbabies,
and plump pearl garlands. Nearby, a
bunch of ornaments mark time in a fish-
bowl, and a sweet faded cotton stocking
hangs at the fireplace. But the eye cannot
resist the still life poised in the window
against a backdrop of chilly sky. Father
Christmas, fashionable in a long winter
white frock coat, seems to be plodding
in from the cold under the caring eyes of

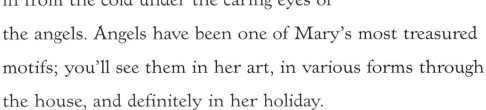

the angels. Angels have been one of Mary's most treasured
motifs; you'll see them in her art, in various forms through
the house, and definitely in her holiday.

Christmas with **Mary**

THE MORE THE MERRIER

Ask an expert (perhaps one of the decorators of famous holiday shopfronts) the criteria for a dazzling window design and you'll probably hear about the clarity of a single vision and harmony among the elements, It is with her well-loved spirit of mischief then that Mary mounts many of her visual entertainments completely and blissfully ignoring all these rules. In the deep window frames of the living room, Father Christmas is surrounded by a chorus of angels, a veil of snowflakes—no two of these are alike!—drifts of snow, and ropes of crystal beads.

REFLECTION OF A SNOWBABY

Sweet vignettes, particularly those featuring snow pixies, are a Mary trademark, as much at Christmas as any time during the year. A fine example is the adorable figurine astride a snow-frosted sprig of pine. Mary's tucked the pieces into a mirror frame, so that the beauty of the arrangement is twice as intriguing.

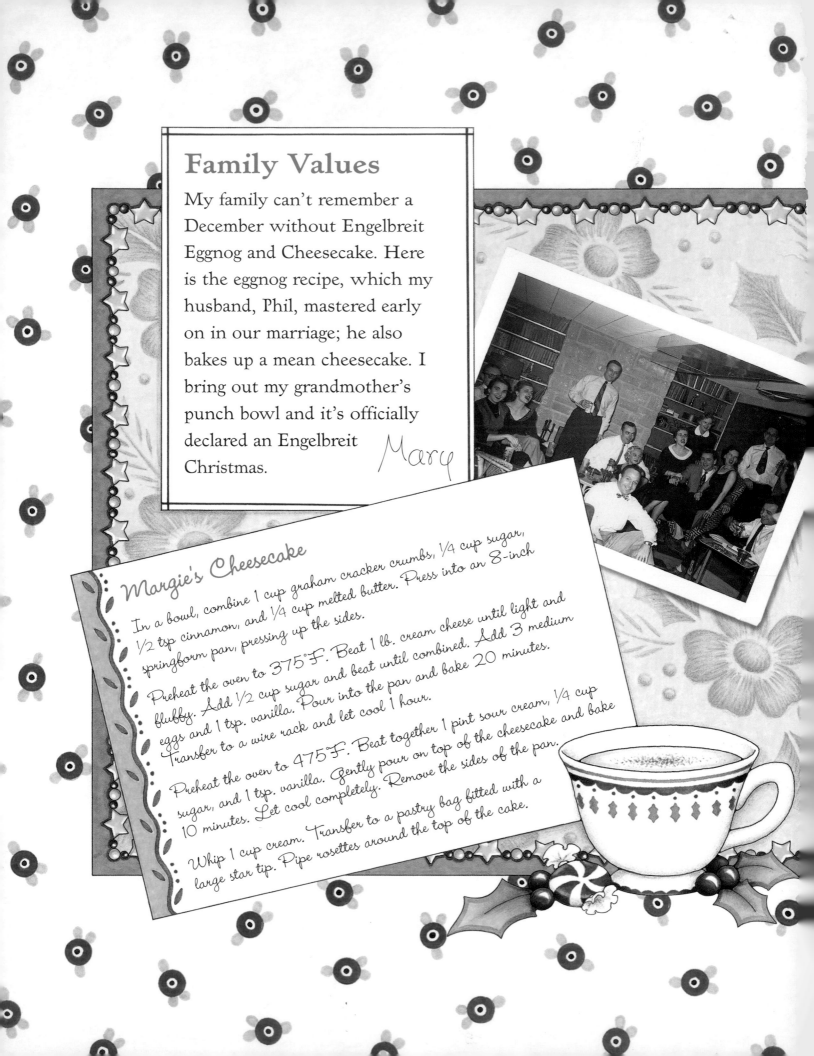

Family Values

My family can't remember a December without Engelbreit Eggnog and Cheesecake. Here is the eggnog recipe, which my husband, Phil, mastered early on in our marriage; he also bakes up a mean cheesecake. I bring out my grandmother's punch bowl and it's officially declared an Engelbreit Christmas.

Mary

Margie's Cheesecake

In a bowl, combine 1 cup graham cracker crumbs, 1/4 cup sugar, 1/2 tsp cinnamon, and 1/4 cup melted butter. Press into an 8-inch springform pan, pressing up the sides.

Preheat the oven to 375°F. Beat 1 lb. cream cheese until light and fluffy. Add 1/2 cup sugar and beat until combined. Add 3 medium eggs and 1 tsp. vanilla. Pour into the pan and bake 20 minutes. Transfer to a wire rack and let cool 1 hour.

Preheat the oven to 475°F. Beat together 1 pint sour cream, 1/4 cup sugar, and 1 tsp. vanilla. Gently pour on top of the cheesecake and bake 10 minutes. Let cool completely. Remove the sides of the pan.

Whip 1 cup cream. Transfer to a pastry bag fitted with a large star tip. Pipe rosettes around the top of the cake.

THE BEST
EGG NOG

1 Dozen Eggs (separated)
1 Quart Bourbon
6 oz. Dark Rum
2 Cups Sugar
2 Quarts Milk (64 oz.)
1 Pint Whipping Cream

Beat egg yolks. Add bourbon and rum
very slowly while beating constantly. Add
sugar and milk to mixture while beating.

Beat egg whites until slightly stiff
and add to yolk mixture.

Beat whipping cream until creamy
and add to other mixture. Serve.

Too MUCH of ANYTHING is BAD, BUT Too MUCH WHISKEY is JUST ENOUGH.
•MARK TWAIN•

Christmas Eve at Last

Supper for Santa

A most delicious conclusion to the countdown!

Silent night, holy night, all is calm, all is bright. . . . Your Christmas Eve is probably not silent at all, nor is everyone calm. Give in to the mood of excitement and encourage the household to share the merriment. Whatever your personal tradition—some families wait until this night to decorate the tree; many folks attend midnight services—it can only be enhanced by a spectacular supper. Just the idea of supper appeals; unlike the more formal holiday dinners, this meal should be comfortable and informal but still a bit special. With this in mind, we've created a menu that will satisfy sophisticated guests as well as

those looking for food that is as much fun as the holiday. Everything can be made ahead, then served just as soon as all that last-minute wrapping is completed.

Supper begins with some unusual cheese puffs: baguette slices topped with cheese and mayonnaise, and baked until they're golden. The star of the meal is a hearty, scrumptious beef stew from Greece. It simmers quietly during the afternoon flurry of activity, then is served with hot buttered noodles. Vegetables are still important, even on December 24th, and green beans keep us healthy and in tip-top form for opening gifts. As for dessert, a heart-pounding ice cream bombe, decorated with meringue stars and green licorice, is dramatically presented atop a pedestal stand. Is Christmas great or what?

A RED & GREEN SUPPER BEFORE SANTA'S VISIT

Stifado, a delicious Greek-inspired stew scented with rosemary, is stick-to-your-ribs good on Christmas eve. With it, fresh, homemade biscuits are just special enough. Begin the meal with a tray of warm cheese puffs and finish with a heavenly ice cream bombe that will invite lovely visions of sugarplums to your dreams PANTRY **PAGE 94**

Eat heavy and sleep soundly, for tomorrow's **Christmas!**

Last-Minute Preparations for a Wondrous Morning

DRESS FOR SUCCESS

Here, finally, is the evening of December 24th, just a few hours from the thrill of Christmas morning. A few hours, but critical hours. Be sure to grab Santa's attention; for these last precious moments, make preparations in a holiday shirt that can bring only luck. A fresh T-shirt, complete with an iron-on photo transfer and a band of rickrack stitched to the collar should do the job.

BE KIND TO ANIMALS

Remember the gentle creatures who work with Santa. How thoughtful it is to offer the reindeer a few munchies to enjoy as they wait for the Boss to fill the stockings and sort the presents under the tree. Try a crispy cereal in a glass jar. Cover the lid with fabric and ribbon; the breeze will tinkle the jingle bells.

It's Never Too Late

For kids who've been both naughty and nice, a few last-chance efforts couldn't help but encourage Santa's generosity. These handy ideas will be invaluable. And they can be done before midnight.

Reindeer Food
(If You Flew & Flew &
Flew all night, You'd
Too work up an
appetite!)
Sprinkle Generously on lawn
CHRISTMAS Eve!

LIGHT SANTA'S WAY

In the midst of all his hard work, how terrible it would be if Santa were to take a tumble in your dark living room! Show your consideration with a custom shade on an inexpensive plug-in night-light. These are handy too for hallways when restless insomniacs can't resist peeking downstairs to see if Santa's come yet.

WORKSHOP **PAGE 129**

HONESTY IS THE BEST POLICY, BUT CAN IT HURT TO BURNISH THE TRUTH A BIT?

If you're worried that Santa may be getting to your home toward the end of a busy night, take no chances. Grab his attention big-time with these appealing dishes. Heap the dishes with the most excellent cookies and beverage that can be found! WORKSHOP **PAGE 128**

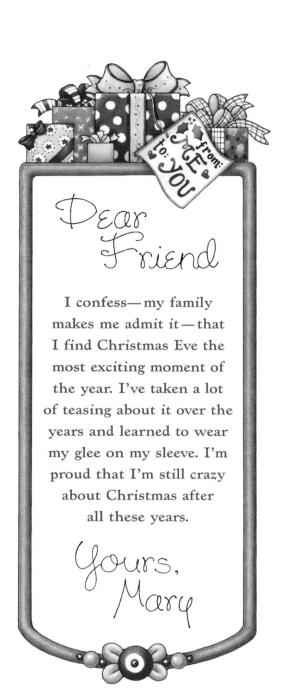

Dear Friend

I confess—my family makes me admit it—that I find Christmas Eve the most exciting moment of the year. I've taken a lot of teasing about it over the years and learned to wear my glee on my sleeve. I'm proud that I'm still crazy about Christmas after all these years.

Yours, Mary

...and to all a good night!

Joy to the World

It's good to be children
sometimes, and never better
than at Christmas.

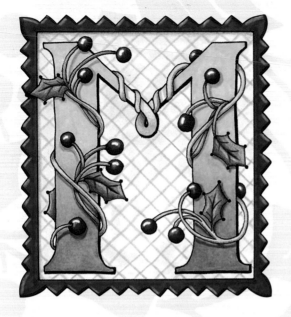

ay peace and happiness be yours! Along with good company, good presents, and good treats! May the day begin with choruses of delight and close in an oasis of calm. And may your blessings outnumber your problems, if only by one.

Christmas Day is time together enjoying all the celebrations and preparations, joys and chores, the presents and surprises, and ribbons and gift wrap and tissue paper scattered all over. If you crave order and your family is oblivious, let it go and consider your gift to them a day of carefree chaos.

CHRISTMAS IS COMING

Previous page: If Santa were going to trade in his old sleigh and give the reindeer early retirement, this cherry-red pick-up would be just the ticket. The truck is so much roomier that there is space for all the presents and the tree! Not everyone can back a pick-up like this out of the barn, but whatever your bumper is attached to, it can proclaim JOY to one and all. Imagine arriving at the children's wing of the hospital or a seniors' home in this beauty. ❖ WORKSHOP **PAGE 131** Opposite: Deliver an unforgettable Christmas breakfast to someone whose celebration has been been made modest by circumstances. Think of a pretty hatbox, gaily painted outside and overflowing with sweet, thoughtful little luxuries nestled within curly white excelsior. Painting the box needn't be more elaborate than simple stripes in chirpy colors, with a message at the bottom.

Something—batteries, grape juice, ornament hooks—will have been forgotten. Make a contest and award first prize to the person who correctly predicts what it will be, then laugh about it.

During the day, let conversation float from one pleasant topic to another. Here is a rare opportunity to spend a few minutes with everyone, to be sure they know that you value their contribution to the holiday and their presence—and their presents.

Christmas
with Mary

Christmas morning for Mary has

always been a time of exceptional excitement
and unabashed gratification. As a girl growing
up with her two sisters, Mary was known
as the earlybird, a term all too familiar to
every sleep-starved parent. Luckily for us,
Mary's rapture for anything that has to do
with Christmas has kept pace with her life,
and thousands of drawings, cards, figurines,
decorations, and sentiments later, homes
nationwide reflect Mary's influence in their holiday.

Is this passion for Christmas a gift that might be passed
across the generations? Mary is about to find out,
as she opens her home to her granddaughter,
Mikayla, and her chum Lydia, a formidable two-
year-old twosome at the peak of their Christmas
prowess. Truly, there will never be a better
opportunity to let innocence and joy prevail.
Baby, it's Christmas!

Christmas with **Mary,** starring Mikayla and Lydia

A COUPLE OF YOUNG PRINCESSES

Happily, Mikayla has made her grandparents' Christmas wish come true. Together with her pal Lydia, they share breakfast, after adorning themselves in regal crowns. Mikayla chose green gemstones, and Lydia went for red. How appropriate the crowns for the two little princesses.  WORKSHOP **PAGE 131**

See **Christmas** through the eyes of children

A HOUSE OF DREAMS

Mary's little pottery bungalow is one of her most adored possessions, and each year it is among the first pieces to get a holiday look, protected by a glass bell jar with a Christmas thought tied on with ribbon. When, after years of searching, Mary discovered the real house of her dreams, the resemblance to this cottage was uncanny (though the house itself is quite a bit larger).

I want a house
that has got over
all its troubles;
I don't want to
spend the rest of
my life bringing
up a young
and inexperienced
house.

—J.K. JEROME

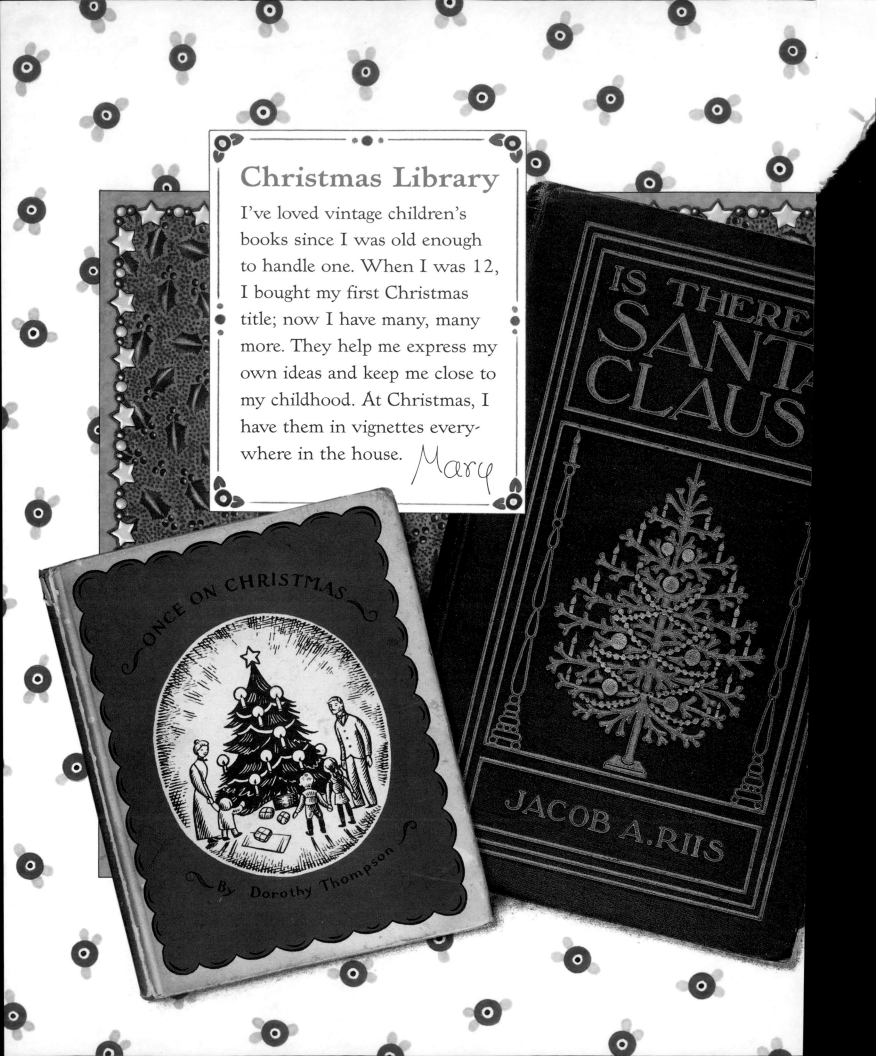

Christmas Library

I've loved vintage children's books since I was old enough to handle one. When I was 12, I bought my first Christmas title; now I have many, many more. They help me express my own ideas and keep me close to my childhood. At Christmas, I have them in vignettes everywhere in the house. *Mary*

ONCE ON CHRISTMAS

By Dorothy Thompson

IS THERE A SANTA CLAUS

JACOB A. RIIS

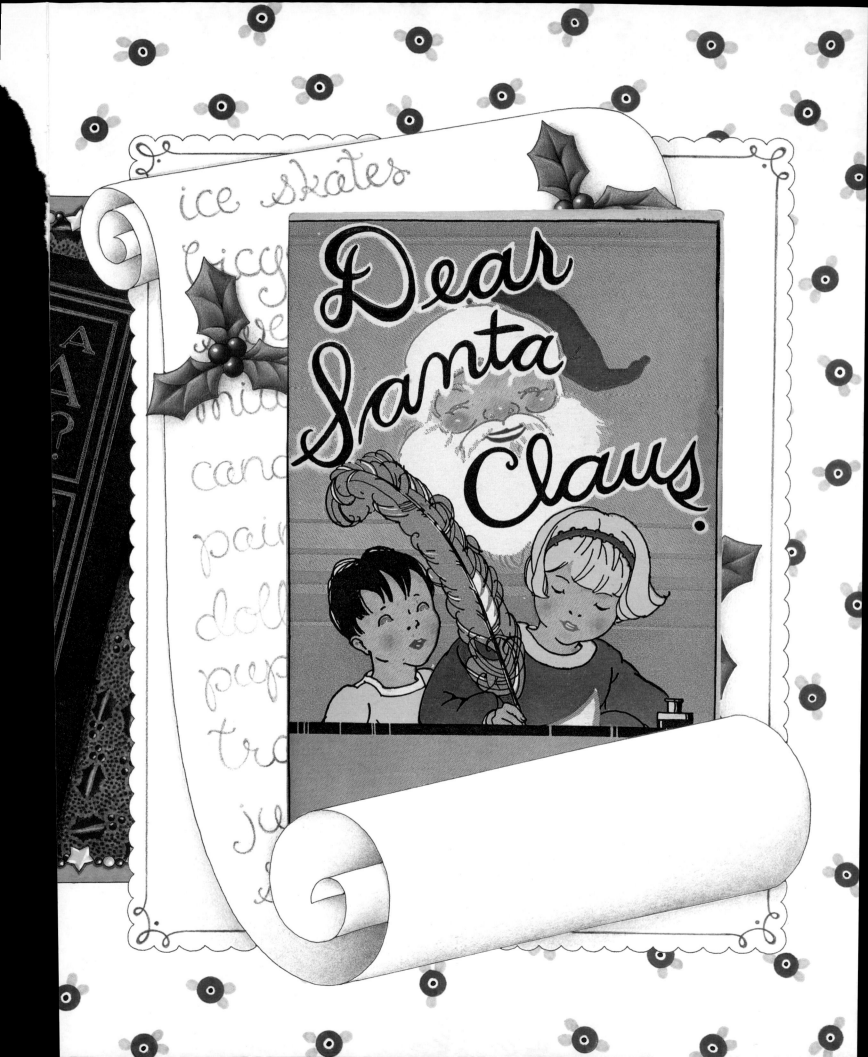

The Best BREAKFAST EVER

We heard the bells
on Christmas morn,
their old familiar
carols play.

Get up, get up, get out of bed—Let's go see if Santa has been here! If it's Mary's house, chances are pretty good the old gent has been there and made a stop in every room. Two young girls wash up, then, there on the bedpost, they find Christmas crowns to don for the journey downstairs to the tree, the presents, and the best breakfast of the year. It's so exciting!

To begin December 25th, the perfect meal is one that is special and fun, of course, but it can adapt itself to your holiday timetable. Serve breakfast wherever you think your family will most enjoy it, whether that happens to be the dining

room with a splendid tree in the corner, the living room or family room with their relaxed environments, or as Mary and her husband, Phil, do, in the kitchen, the warm and cozy and fabulously decorated kitchen.

Chef Phil has assembled most of the meal earlier; the white chocolate muffins with fresh raspberries, sunny orange juice, and gelatin for the marshmallow parfaits can be prepared the day before.

When folks feel the need to refuel, attention turns to the business of eating. Phil wraps crescents of honeydew melon with frizzled ham, then whips up a main-course omelette stuffed with golden cheddar cheese and sautéed mushrooms. Laughter and excitement resound at the table, then every-one heads back to the Christmas morning routine: presents, presents, presents.

ANGELS GATHER

The round kitchen table, hub of daily family life, is conveniently within sight of the Christmas tree in the den. Cherry, cream, marshmallow and walnut parfaits take longer to pronounce than they do to make (or eat!). For this break-fast, they make a light, colorful dessert.

PANTRY **PAGE 115**

"I knew **I was good,** but I didn't realize I'd **been that good all year!"**

Take Inspiration

Is anybody surprised that scores of Scotties show up for the Engelbreit Christmas?

Don't limit yourself to holiday symbols; play with stuff you really love. Like Scotties, from an appliqué napkin in  a no-sew curtain to yummy black licorice Scotties in a Candyland garland. Then there is the real deal: after all his hard work and good behavior, dapper Henry keeps close watch over the festivities. But the real Christmas morning scene-stealer is a Scottie puppy.

This little fellow is about to make chaos of the holiday papers under the tree. We dare you to top that!

IT'S STILL A SURPRISE

A recent survey said nearly seven of every ten dog owners planned to buy canine presents at Christmas. There are two ways to look at that: some will buy gifts for their canines, while others will buy canines as gifts.

Every dog has his day, and why shouldn't it be Christmas? A snazzy new collar, customized with gingham, gold rickrack, snowflakes, and embroidered with the dog's name, is a sure thing. Such couture finery is only a temporary distraction from the super present—a Scottie puppy! This young fellow, just about as black as coal, looks ready to take on his new life. Tune in next year to see how he's doing!

Sugarplum Heaven

Sweet Dreams

A Christmas Day Visit to Candyland

Gifts might be more than a stocking can hold, even more than the biggest gift box will contain. An example? How about a private Candyland, one room devoted to the love of candy. Unveil this treat on Christmas day, once the presents have been opened and symptoms of the inevitable letdown appear.

You can put together a Candyland in different pieces at your convenience during the holidays, then install it all in about an hour. Choose a focal point: in this case, a mirror claims front and center, cleverly reflecting the decorations set before it. Write your greeting on the mirror, together with

a handful of candy flourishes (these are cellophane-wrapped peppermints, but could just as well be sour balls, tiny candycanes, or short lengths of ribbon candy). Hang a wreath covered in peppermints from a mossy green velvet ribbon, then string a candy garland across the mirror frame.

Time to set the best table of the day! The perfect holiday cloth is a vintage candy-print cotton, but any festive fabric will do. Let unframed mirrors suggest skating ponds and frilly lace doilies be snow. Bring in the candy decorations and position them in order of size. Begin with the bigger ones, then add on bit by bit: a peppermint and gumdrop topiary, a tiny tree draped in candy garlands, a background of big lollipops. Tuck in little Christmas houses, a forest of bottlebrush trees, and some soft lights. Let it glow, let it glow, let it glow.

SHARE A CUP OF CHEER

To mimic hot chocolate, a peppermint cup was filled with nondairy creamer. You'll see something like this only at Christmas, and only in Candyland, where all candy is taken seriously. Let no one say there can be too much of a good thing.

Better than a winter wonderland, it's the **Christmas Candyland!**

CANDYLAND CONCEPT

Little houses on a mirror dusted with snow, backed by an enormous pot with a broomstick tree draped in candy—in theory, it makes no sense; in person, everyone is enchanted at its sight. Take a trip to the candy shop; toss logic to the wind and select whatever candies are appealing. Back home, grab a bunch of leftover decorations, silly statues, fake snow, and some dreamy lighting. Now, you're on your way to Candyland! **WORKSHOP PAGE 134-135**

Just Add Love
Holiday
Candles make festivities even more jolly, and they are economical options when lighting your rooms. Look for ordinary inexpensive poured candles in glass containers. Decorate the glass with lots of scrap paper, little bits of trim, ball fringe, buttons, and jingle bells.

pantry

Here's food for the holidays that's better than good—it's the best: divine biscuits, succulent roasts, second-helping vegetables, yummy cookies, scrumptious candies.

We have some favorites, like a stunning crown roast, new treats like cherry cream-marshmallow-walnut parfaits—imagine, dessert at Christmas breakfast!—and we've got a snack for Santa that will make your home his favorite stop.

Holiday Pantry

Before the holidays arrive, there are a number of items that are handy to keep in your pantry for guests who just drop by, for extra dinner guests, and for making entertaining generally easier. With these on hand you will be able to create quick hors d'oeuvres, easy side dishes to stretch dinner, and many, many wonderful desserts.

Plenty of olives

Cornichons

Cheeses: Parmesan, extra-sharp Cheddar, Boursin, and a blue cheese

Hard salamis

Specialty crackers

Frozen homemade pasta sauce

Frozen puff pastry

Ice creams and sorbets

Walnuts, unshelled pistachios, almonds, salted peanuts, and macadamias

Chocolates: unsweetened, bittersweet, semisweet, milk and white

Miniature chocolate chips

Shredded coconut

Crystallized ginger

Miniature marshmallows

Gold and silver dragées

Red and green coarse sugars

Purchased shortbread and ginger cookies

Fudge and caramel sauces

Specialty teas and coffees

The Perfect Partner: Puff Pastry

A few boxes of puff pastry are the best accessory a busy host can have. Quickly and easily shaped into fancy hors d'oeuvres, golden crowns to make a pot pie absolutely regal, and flaky, buttery wraps for any number of sweet fillings, puff pastry is delicious, reliable, and spectacular.

Bare Naked Pfeffernuesse

Spicy and satisfying, Pfeffernuesse are synonymous with the winter holidays. We break style here and leave off the traditional confectioners' sugar coating, but feel free to dredge yours if you prefer historical accuracy.

1 ½ cups flour
1 teaspoon cinnamon
½ teaspoon ground
    cardamom
¼ teaspoon ground cloves
¼ teaspoon ground nutmeg
⅛ teaspoon freshly ground
    black pepper
¼ teaspoon baking powder
⅛ teaspoon baking soda
¼ teaspoon salt
3 tablespoons light or dark molasses
3 tablespoons brandy
¼ cup (½ stick) unsalted butter, at room temperature
½ cup sugar
1 egg yolk
¼ cup blanched slivered almonds, finely chopped
¼ cup chopped dried apricots
1 teaspoon finely grated lemon zest

1. In a large bowl, sift together the flour, cinnamon, cardamom, cloves, nutmeg, pepper, baking powder, baking soda, and salt.

2. In a small bowl, combine the molasses and brandy.

3. In the large bowl of an electric mixer at medium-high speed, beat the butter and sugar until the mixture is light and fluffy. Scrape down the side of the bowl. Add the egg yolk and beat until well combined.

4. On low speed, add the flour mixture alternating with the molasses mixture, beginning and ending with the flour mixture. Add the almonds, dried apricots and zest, beating just until combined. Press the mixture into a disk, wrap in plastic, and refrigerate at least 8 hours or overnight.

5. Preheat the oven to 350°F. Grease 2 baking sheets.

6. Roll the dough into ¾-inch balls and place on the prepared baking sheet about 1 inch apart.

7. Bake the cookies 12 to 14 minutes, or until they are light golden. Let cool on the baking sheet on a wire rack for 4 minutes. Transfer to the wire rack and let cool completely. **Makes 3 dozen**

Baker's Note Another tempting disguise for Pfeffernuesse is an orange-flavored glaze. Mix confectioners' sugar with orange juice and a bit of zest or Grand Marnier to a thinner-than-spreading consistency. Brush warm cookies with the glaze and allow to dry completely. Whichever way you prefer them—or create an assortment of all three—Pfeffernuesse are hardy little travelers.

Chewy Chocolate Brown Sugar Cookies

Chewy, gooey, good and big! is the reaction you will get from all your guests as they delight in these mounds of chocolate heaven. Make the cookies smaller if you wish, but whatever you do, make a double batch.

- ½ **cup flour**
- ¼ **teaspoon baking powder**
- ¼ **teaspoon salt**
- 1 **pound semisweet chocolate, chopped**
- ¼ **cup (½ stick) unsalted butter, at room temperature**
- ¾ **cup firmly packed light or dark brown sugar**
- 2 **large eggs**
- 1 **teaspoon vanilla**
- 2 **cups chopped walnuts**

1. Preheat the oven to 350°F. In a medium bowl, combine the flour, baking powder, and salt.

2. In a double boiler over gently simmering water, melt half the chocolate. Remove from the heat and set aside.

3. In the large bowl of an electric mixer at medium speed, beat the butter, brown sugar, eggs, and vanilla until light and fluffy. Add the melted chocolate and mix with a wooden spoon until smooth.

4. With the mixer on low speed, gradually add the flour mixture and beat just until combined. Add the reserved chopped chocolate and the nuts. Drop ¼ cupfuls of the dough onto ungreased baking sheets about 2 inches apart.

5. Bake the cookies 12 to 13 minutes, or until they are puffed and set. Cool the cookies on the baking sheets for 1 minute, then transfer to wire racks to cool completely. **Makes about 1 dozen**

A favorite Mary cookie is about to make a mouth very happy.

May All Your Christmas Dreams Be Chocolate

*Chocolate needs no endorsements from Mary Engelbreit;
no matter what its form; unsweetened, bittersweet, semisweet, milk
or white, we just can't get enough of the stuff. During the holidays,
we look to our chocolate cupboards as inspiration for luscious
concoctions, many of them created at the last minute.*

Simple truffles These melt-in-your-mouth delicacies are outrageously expensive at the candy shop, but without their fancy "couverture" coating, they are simplicity itself to make. In a pot over medium-high heat, bring 6 tablespoons of heavy cream to a boil, then pour the cream over 12 ounces of chopped semisweet chocolate. Let sit for 1 minute; stir to combine. Add 1/2 cup softened unsalted butter and stir to combine. Add chopped nuts, miniature marshmallows, or bits of crushed cookies. Cover with plastic wrap and refrigerate just until firm. Roll teaspoon-size pieces into balls. Roll the balls in sifted cocoa, toasted ground nuts, or shredded coconut.

Chocolate Greetings When you care enough to send the very tastiest, melt 2 ounces chocolate. Transfer to a resealable plastic bag and snip off the bottom corner of the bag to make a small hole. Pipe out holiday messages onto plates, then add the desserts. How to perfect your skills? Practice (consume result), practice (consume result), practice!

Swanky S'mores We like our S'mores in more than one version. A favorite is based on replacing the graham crackers, which don't really hold up their end of the sweet triangle anyway. Shortbread, buttery, rich shortbread, is our choice. When it's combined with marshmallows and dark chocolate, you're one step closer to heaven.

Christmas Perfection

Melt white chocolate and mix in maraschino cherries and unsalted pistachio nuts. Drop by spoonful on waxed paper and allow to set.

Grilled Chocolate Sandwiches

Between slices of white bread, place a piece of chocolate the thickness of a Hershey bar. Spread the outsides of the bread sides with unsalted butter. Heat a small skillet. Add the sandwich and cook until golden on one side; flip, cook to melt the chocolate, and serve immediately.

Chocolate Bliss

Thank the brilliant Engelbreit kitchen for these little bits of joy. At room temperature, the chocolate concoction is a little like a sublime fudge but without the work; when it's warm, it's as spreadable as peanut butter. Melt 1 pound chocolate with 3/4 cup cream, stir to combine. Remove from the heat and cool. Stir in 2 tablespoons of liqueur—coconut, orange, coffee, creme de menthe. Pour the mixture into a 9-inch square pan and chill. When it's cold, cut the mixture into blocks or use miniature cookie cutters to create shapes. Plop one into a big mug of steaming hot coffee and you'll take the chill off!

Chocolate Dips

Melt chocolate and dip away: Nut brittle, either homemade or from the candy store, is even better when it's been dipped in chocolate. Fabulous strawberries are in the shops at Christmastime, along with cherries, apricots, and clementines. If your family fancies candied orange and grapefruit peels, enhance them with a dark chocolate bath. Candied ginger loves chocolate too. Set the dipped fruit on wire racks to allow the chocolate to dry; meanwhile, use the microwave to melt some white chocolate in a small plastic bag. Snip a corner off the bag and drizzle white chocolate over the dark.

Double Frosty Brownies

Get your frost fix with brownies lavished with chocolate frosting, then covered with chilly peppermint crumbles. These are so quick and simple don't bother to get out the electric mixer.

1 cup cake flour
2 tablespoons unsweetened cocoa,
    preferably Dutch-process
½ teaspoon salt
5 ounces unsweetened
    chocolate
¾ cup (1½ sticks)
    unsalted butter
1½ cups sugar
3 large eggs, beaten
1 teaspoon vanilla
¾ teaspoon peppermint extract
½ cup finely chopped bittersweet chocolate
Your favorite creamy chocolate frosting
Crushed peppermint sticks, for garnish

kids can do it!

1. Preheat the oven to 350°F. Generously butter and flour an 8-inch square pan.

2. Sift together the flour, cocoa, and salt. Set aside.

3. In the top of a double boiler over gently simmering water, melt the chocolate and butter. Pour the mixture into a large mixing bowl and let cool 5 minutes, stirring occasionally. Add the sugar and stir until combined. Add the eggs and beat until well combined.

4. Stir in the flour mixture, mixing just until combined. Stir in the vanilla and peppermint extract. Stir in the chopped chocolate until evenly distributed. Pour the batter into the prepared pan and spread evenly.

5. Bake the brownies 30 to 40 minutes, or until a toothpick inserted in the center comes out almost clean. Let cool for 10 minutes on a wire rack.

6. Remove the brownies from the pan. Spread with chocolate frosting; sprinkle with the candies. Cut into squares. **Makes 8**

Melt-in-Your-Mouth Butter Crescents

These buttery cookies are crowd pleasers and kid pleasers; little fingers are adept at rolling and shaping.

1 cup (2 sticks) unsalted butter, at room temperature
1½ cups flour
½ teaspoon salt
¼ cup ground walnuts
½ cup confectioners' sugar

1. Preheat the oven to 275°F. In the bowl of an electric mixer at low speed, beat the butter, flour, salt, and nuts until combined. Increase the speed to medium and beat until smooth.

2. Shape teaspoonfuls into crescents and place an inch apart on an ungreased baking sheet.

3. Bake the cookies 10 to 15 minutes, or until they are set; do not brown. Meanwhile, sift the confectioners' sugar onto a plate. While the cookies are still warm, roll them in the confectioners' sugar. Carefully transfer to a serving platter. **Makes 1 dozen**

Peppermint Patsies

No baking required! Pleading for the recipe is what you can expect from lucky friends. Present the precious patsies nestled in a cellophane bag, tied with a red ribbon.

- 1 pound confectioners' sugar
- 3 tablespoons unsalted butter, softened
- 1 tablespoon peppermint extract
- ½ teaspoon vanilla
- ¼ teaspoon salt
- ¼ cup evaporated milk
- 2 cups semisweet chocolate chips
- 2 tablespoons vegetable shortening
- 2 ounces white chocolate, chopped
- Small red candies, for decorating

1. Cover a wire rack with waxed paper and set aside. In the large bowl of an electric mixer at medium speed, beat the sugar, butter, peppermint extract, vanilla, and salt until combined. Add the milk and mix well.

2. Roll the dough into 1-inch balls and place on an ungreased baking sheet. Refrigerate 20 minutes. Using a clean glass with a flat bottom, flatten each ball to a ¼-inch thickness. Refrigerate 30 minutes longer, then freeze for 10 minutes.

3. Meanwhile, in a double boiler over gently simmering water, melt the semisweet chocolate and the shortening; stir until smooth. Let cool for 10 minutes.

4. Dip the patsies into the chocolate mixture, turning to completely coat. Place the patsies on the prepared wire rack. Freeze for 5 minutes to harden the chocolate.

5. In a double boiler over gently simmering water, melt the white chocolate. Transfer to a resealable plastic bag. Snip off a tiny corner of the bag. Drizzle the patsies with the white chocolate. Sprinkle with the red candies and let set. **Makes 2 dozen**

No More Cookie Cowtow

Don't let recipes boss you around. If you love orange, add fresh zest to your favorite recipe. Fancy sandwich cookies? Sandwich your favorite cookies around vanilla frosting, marshmallow cream, or peanut butter. How about rainbow sprinkles? Brush cookies with a thin royal icing and sprinkle to your heart's delight!

Sneaky Chocolate Cherry Sandwiches

Amid a sea of dark and milk chocolate, white chocolate always sounds a note of sophistication. We've slipped it inside cherry sandwiches as one of the best things in life: a chocolate surprise.

1 cup (2 sticks)
   unsalted butter,
   softened
2/3 cup sugar
1 large egg
2 teaspoons vanilla
2 1/3 cups flour
1/4 teaspoon baking
   powder
1/4 teaspoon salt
3/4 cup finely chopped white chocolate, melted
1/2 cup cherry jam

1. Preheat the oven to 400°F. In the large bowl of an electric mixer at medium-high speed, beat the butter and sugar until light and fluffy. Add the egg and vanilla and beat until combined.

2. Sift together the flour, baking powder and salt. On low speed, beat the flour mixture into the butter mixture. Roll the dough between sheets of waxed paper to a ¼-inch thickness. Refrigerate 30 minutes, until firm.

3. With a small cookie cutter, cut out rounds; the scraps should be rerolled. Bake the cookies 6 to 8 minutes until just set. Cool completely on a wire rack.

4. Spread a small amount of the white chocolate on the bottoms of half the cookies. Set aside.

5. In a medium bowl, beat the cherry jam until smooth. Spread a small amount of the jam on the bottoms of the remaining half of the cookies and top with the white-chocolate covered cookies, top side up.
Makes about 2 dozen

Four Tips for Cookie Exchange Greatness

1

Pick a date convenient for everyone working around family time.

2

Decide if the exchange is open to non-baking family members and friends, or just to the bakers? The answer will affect how many cookies you'll need.

3

Think about the selection. If anyone asks what cookie to bring, ask for something unusual; there will be plenty of chocolate chippers (not that that's a bad thing!).

4

Plan the table to make the cookies look fabulous; pull out pedestals, holiday decorations, good lighting.

Sparkle-Plenty Cookies

*Baked right on lollipop sticks,
these are delicious cookies, and they're
just as good as festive decorations.*

2 cups flour

½ teaspoon baking powder

¼ teaspoon salt

**10 tablespoons (1¼ sticks) unsalted butter,
    at room temperature**

¾ cup plus 2 tablespoons granulated sugar

1 large egg

1½ teaspoons vanilla

Favorite vanilla frosting, for decorating

Colored coarse sugar or sanding sugar, for decorating

1. In a medium bowl, whisk together the flour, baking powder, and salt.

2. In the large bowl of an electric mixer at medium-high speed, beat the butter and granulated sugar until the mixture is light and fluffy. Beat in the egg and vanilla until they are completely combined.

3. On low speed, slowly add the flour mixture, beating just until incorporated. Divide the dough into 4 pieces. Shape each piece into a disk and wrap in plastic. Place the disks in the refrigerator about 1 hour or up to 2 days.

4. Preheat the oven to 350°F. On a lightly floured surface, roll out 1 piece of dough to a ⅛-inch thickness. Cut out stars, using assorted-size cookie cutters and place 2 inches apart on ungreased baking sheets. Insert one 8-inch lollipop stick into each star, pressing to make sure the sticks are secure but not poking through the other side. The dough scraps should be chilled and rerolled.

5. Bake the cookies 8 to 10 minutes, or until the edges are lightly browned. Cool 1 to 2 minutes on the baking sheets on wire racks, then transfer carefully to wire racks to cool completely.

6. With a small knife, frost the tops of the cookies. Gently sprinkle the cookies with the colored sugar; let set for 30 minutes.

Makes about 2 dozen

THE MORE THE MERRIER

Spree of Spritz Cookies

No Christmas party is complete without spritz cookies. We have gone with the traditional red, green and white, but feel free to make a rainbow of colors.

1 cup (2 sticks)
   unsalted butter, at
   room temperature
1 cup granulated sugar
1 large egg
2 ½ cups flour
¾ teaspoon salt
1 ½ teaspoons
   vanilla
Red and green food coloring
Colored sugars, red and green round jelly candies,
   mini chocolate-covered candies, and white
   sprinkles, for decorating

1. Preheat the oven to 400°F. In the large bowl of an electric mixer at medium speed, beat the butter and sugar until light and fluffy. Beat in the egg.

2. On low speed, gradually add the flour and salt, beating just until combined. Beat in the vanilla.

3. Divide the dough into 3 pieces and place each in a bowl. Add red food coloring to 1 dough and knead to combine. Add green food coloring to 1 dough and knead to combine.

4. Transfer the white dough to a cookie press fitted with the desired disk. Press out the dough onto an ungreased cookie sheet. Transfer the red dough to the cookie press fitted with the desired disk. Press out the dough onto an ungreased cookie sheet. Using a clean cookie press and disk, press out the green dough onto an ungreased cookie sheet. Decorate the cookies however you like.

5. Bake the spritz 6 to 9 minutes, or until they are set but not brown. Transfer to a wire rack to cool. **Makes about 5 dozen**

Tender Almond Golddust Amaretti

Heavenly, with a melt-in-your-mouth sweetness, homemade amaretti feature gold baubles.

4 large eggs
2 cups granulated sugar
One 2-ounce bottle almond extract
6 cups ground almonds
1 ½ cups confectioners' sugar
Gold dragées, for garnish

1. Preheat the oven to 350°F. Line 2 large baking sheets with parchment paper and set aside.

2. In the large bowl of an electric mixer at medium speed, beat the eggs, granulated sugar, and almond extract until they are completely combined. Add the almonds and blend well.

3. Drop the batter by teaspoonfuls onto the prepared baking sheets 1½ inches apart.

4. Bake the cookies 8 to 10 minutes, or until they are light golden brown; do not overbake. Transfer to wire racks.

5. As soon as the cookies are cool enough to handle, dredge them in sifted confectioners' sugar. Add gold dragées. **Makes 2 dozen**

Snow Blush

Serve these sweet light cocktails in pretty champagne flutes. In place of the Champagne, you might try Prosecco, a sparkling Italian wine that is not as sweet as Asti Spumante.

1 cup cranberry juice cocktail, cold
1 bottle Champagne, cold

Pour the cranberry juice into flutes, filling each only half full. Top with Champagne, and stir gently to combine. Serve immediately.

Serves 6

Martini Breezes

Sometimes, there is just nothing as smooth as a perfectly concocted martini. With a myriad of flavor choices, we have narrowed ours down to a Christmasy peppermint.

Crushed ice
1 cup vodka
¼ cup peppermint schnapps
1 cup ice cubes
6 peppermint candies, for garnish

1. Fill martini glasses with crushed ice and set aside.

2. In a pitcher, combine the vodka, schnapps and ice. Stir gently. Discard the ice from the glasses and strain the martini mixture into the glasses. Drop 1 peppermint candy in each glass. Serve immediately. **Serves 6**

A Season of High Spirits

Here are some tips for setting up a holiday bar:

1. Don't even try to have all the ingredients for every cocktail. Have a specialty or two and a choice of wine, beer, and soft drinks.

2. Stock up on mixers: club soda, tonic, ginger ale, cola, cranberry and orange juice.

3. If you really want to get fancy, offer a liqueur or brandy as an after-dinner drink.

4. Remember garnishes! Lemon peel, clementine segments, paper-thin slices of pear or apple, cranberries, and candycane stirrers.

Best-Ever Cheese Puffs

Dressed up with red tomatoes and green arugula, these crunchy toasts signal that the holidays have begun.

4 slices bacon, cut into ½-inch-thick pieces

1 tablespoon olive oil

1 small yellow onion, cut lengthwise into eighths

½ pint grape tomatoes, halved, or cherry tomatoes, quartered

1 teaspoon sugar

2 tablespoons snipped fresh basil

Salt and freshly ground black pepper, to taste

¾ cup grated Cheddar cheese

3 tablespoons mayonnaise

1 baguette, sliced crosswise

Basil, for garnish

1. In a skillet over medium-high heat, cook the bacon until crisp. Transfer to a paper towel-lined plate and crumble.

2. Drain the bacon fat from the skillet and add the olive oil. Add the onion and cook, stirring, until caramelized. Add the tomatoes, bacon, sugar, and basil and cook until heated through. Season with salt and pepper.

3. Preheat the oven to 425°F. In a bowl, mix the cheese and mayonnaise together until combined. Top each baguette slice with cheese mixture. Transfer to a baking sheet and bake about 5 minutes, until the cheese has melted. Transfer to a serving plate and top with a small spoonful of the tomato mixture. Garnish each with a piece of basil. Serve immediately. **Serves 8**

Scents to Savor the Season

Make up a double batch of spice cookie dough. Roll out and shape the dough into cookies, arrange them on baking sheets, and freeze. Wrap unbaked cookies tightly with plastic wrap and foil and keep frozen. When the doorbell announces visitors, it's no trouble at all to bake up a sheet of fresh cookies.

Crown Roast with Apple Cranberry Dressing

Royalty is what your family will feel like when they see this regal pork roast coming toward the table.

2 tablespoons olive oil

1 tablespoon dried thyme

1 tablespoon ground allspice

Salt and freshly ground black pepper, to taste

One 8-pound pork crown roast, bones Frenched and roast tied with string into a "crown" (butcher will prepare)

3 tablespoons unsalted butter

1 cup finely chopped celery

2 cups chopped onions

5 slices hearty bread, crusts removed and cut into 1/2-inch cubes

1 cup cooked wild rice

4 cups finely chopped Granny Smith apples

3/4 cup fresh cranberries

1/4 cup snipped fresh sage

1/4 cup chopped fresh thyme

2 cups chicken broth

1/4 cup apple jelly

Cherries and star anise, for garnish

1. Preheat the oven to 450°F. In a bowl, combine the oil, dried thyme, allspice, 2 teaspoons salt, and 1 teaspoon pepper. Transfer the pork roast to a baking pan and rub all over with the oil mixture. Roast 15 minutes; reduce the oven to 250°F and roast for about 2 1/2 hours, until an instant-read thermometer inserted in the thickest part of the meat reads 150 to 155°F.

2. About 1 hour before the roast is finished cooking, in a skillet over medium-high heat, melt the butter. Add the celery and onions and cook, stirring, about 5 minutes, until softened. Remove from the heat.

3. In a large bowl, combine the bread, wild rice, apples, cranberries, onion mixture, sage, and fresh thyme, and

season with salt and pepper. Add about 1/2 cup chicken broth just to moisten. Transfer to a greased baking dish and bake 45 minutes to 1 hour, or until heated through.

4. About 30 minutes before the roast is done, in a small saucepan, heat the remaining chicken broth. In a small bowl, combine the apple jelly and chicken broth and brush the roast all over with the jelly.

5. Let the hot roast rest, covered with a foil tent, 15 minutes. Use a spoon to remove the fat from the juices in the pan; transfer the juices to a gravy boat. Transfer the roast to a platter and spoon the stuffing into the center. Remove the string before carving. **Serves 8**

Classic Creamed Spinach

No holiday is complete without creamed spinach. Quick and easy to make, this is a favorite busy hostess time-saver.

Three 10-ounce packages frozen spinach, cooked

1/4 cup (1/2 stick) unsalted butter

1/2 cup finely chopped onions

2 cups heavy cream

1/2 teaspoon ground nutmeg

Salt and freshly ground black pepper, to taste

1. Cool the spinach and squeeze out any excess water.

2. In a medium saucepan over medium-high heat, melt the butter. Add the onions and cook for about 4 minutes, or until softened. Add the spinach, cover, and cook just until hot. Reduce the heat to medium-low, add the cream and nutmeg, and season with salt and pepper. Stir just until hot. Transfer to a serving bowl. **Serves 8**

Golden Squash Dinghies

Bright orange, baked to tender and sweet perfection, this cute side dish can be prepared ahead and kept warm until serving time.

2 acorn squash, quartered and seeded
1/4 cup (1/2 stick) unsalted butter
2 tablespoons brown sugar
Salt, to taste
Snipped chives and marigold petals, for garnish

1. Preheat the oven to 400°F. Place the squash in a large baking pan. Add enough water to come up the pan 1/2 inch. Cover with foil and bake the squash 45 minutes, or until tender.

2. Increase the oven to 425°F. In a small pan, melt the butter. Remove from the heat and add the sugar. Remove the squash from the oven and pour off the water. Brush the squash with the butter mixture and season with salt. Return to the oven and bake until heated through and lightly browned. Transfer to a serving platter and garnish with the chives and marigold petals. Serve immediately.
Serves 8

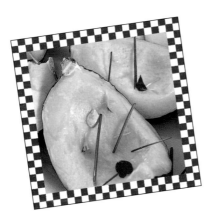

Tricky Turtle Tartlets

Are you ready? Yup, the chocolate is in the bottom of these cute little tartlets. Serve them with dishes of ice cream for extra goodness.

One 8-ounce package cream cheese, softened
1/2 cup (1 stick) unsalted butter, softened
1 cup flour
1 large egg
1/4 teaspoon salt
3/4 cup firmly packed light or dark brown sugar
1 teaspoon vanilla
2/3 cup pecans
24 chunks bittersweet chocolate
Confectioners' sugar, for dusting

1. In the bowl of an electric mixer at medium-high speed, beat the cream cheese and the butter until creamy. Reduce the speed to low and beat in the flour and half the salt. Form the dough into a disk, wrap in plastic, and refrigerate 1 hour.

2. Preheat the oven to 350°F. Generously butter or fit with paper liners 24 muffin pan cups. In a medium bowl, beat the egg and brown sugar. Add the vanilla and the remaining salt and stir until combined. Stir in the nuts.

3. Separate the dough into 24 balls and press into the prepared muffin tins, pressing the dough up the sides. Drop 1 chunk of chocolate in each cup and fill 3/4 full with the filling.

4. Bake the tartlets 25 minutes, until the filling is set. Remove from the pan and transfer to a wire rack to cool. Sift confectioners' sugar over the tops. **Serves 8**

Tasty Can Be Easy

Holiday entertaining can be overwhelming no matter how much time and money you throw at it. But no more: There are a few basic rules for keeping hospitality affordable and enjoyable.

Keep it simple. Basic dishes, ones that are not elaborate or temperamental, will turn out the best, especially when you cook for a crowd. Invest in quality meats from the butcher and choose an easy cooking method. Roasting and stewing are good, when you can put the meat in the pan and that's it.

Once you have the oven going, try to make side dishes or dessert in it. Roast vegetables in the winter, and homemade biscuits are better than everyday potatoes or rice.

Control the menu. Don't cut on the quantities, just on the options. One or two greens, a starch, and a main dish are plenty.

Plan a make-ahead dessert, one that can be baked a week or so in advance and frozen, like a cake or fruit cobbler. If time's run out, layer colorful sorbets with fresh fruit and whipped marscarpone cheese.

A few days before your affair, check that the dishes and utensils are in good order. The table linens should be freshly laundered and pressed, too.

At the beginning of December, order wine, beer, and liqueurs for the entire month. If you don't get enough, you'll have to make more visits to the store, but if you over-order, you can return unopened bottles in January (if you really want to).

Get real about table setting. Amaryllis is wonderful, with fabulous flowers on tall, slender stems that encourage people to chat with their neighbors across the table, and the bulbs last a couple weeks at least. Grab bowls for nuts or vintage glass ornaments. A beautiful cranberry-red bed sheet is perfect for most tables and very affordable. Coil copper wire into napkin rings; top each off with a tiny ornament as a favor.

Keep looking up. Overhead lights can yield powerful looks for decorations from simple to something over the top. Fresh greens, garlands (the kids' construction paper chains), swags of fringes, and paper cones overflowing with tinsel look marvelous. These arrangements will last for days or even weeks.

Stifado with Buttered Noodles

Make this dish the day before you need it and the flavors will improve.

1 teaspoon whole pickling spice
4 pounds boneless chuck
About 1 cup olive oil
16 small onions, peeled
6 bay leaves
½ cup vinegar
One 15½ ounce can
    tomatoes, cut up
7 garlic cloves, finely
    chopped
½ cup red wine
Salt and freshly ground black
    pepper, to taste
About 1 cup tomato juice
One 9-ounce package egg noodles
¼ cup (½ stick) unsalted butter, at room temperature
Rosemary sprigs, for garnish

1. Place the pickling spice in a metal tea ball or tie in a piece of clean cheesecloth.

2. Cut the meat into small pieces. In a large Dutch oven over medium-high heat, heat ¼ cup of oil. Add the meat, in batches, and brown lightly. Move the meat to a platter and set aside; continue browning the remaining meat, adding additional oil as necessary.

3. Return the meat to the Dutch oven, along with any accumulated juices. Add the onions, pickling spice, bay leaves, vinegar, tomatoes, garlic, and wine and season with salt and pepper. Add ¼ cup water. Cover with foil and then with the pot's lid. Cook until the meat is tender and the liquid has a gravy consistency. Immediately remove and discard the pickling spice and bay leaves.

4. Meanwhile, cook the egg noodles according to the manufacturer's directions. Drain, transfer to a serving dish and toss with the butter and season with salt. Spoon the stew over the noodles, garnish with the rosemary sprigs, and serve immediately. **Serves 8**

Green Beans with Toasted Pine Nuts

An alternative to the much-loved green bean casserole, this updated version will delight your guests.

2 pounds green beans, tipped and tailed
5 tablespoons olive oil
¾ cup pine nuts, toasted and finely chopped, plus
    whole toasted nuts, for garnish
Salt and freshly ground black pepper, to taste

1. Cook beans in a large pot of boiling salted water until crisp-tender. Drain and rinse with cold running water.

2. In a large cook pan over medium heat, heat the oil. Add the green beans and cook until just heated through. Stir in the pine nuts and season with salt and pepper. **Serves 8**

Christmas Biscuits

Studded with a burst of sun-dried tomatoes and a sprinkling of fresh parsley, these quick biscuits will soon be on your table every night of the week.

4 1/2 cups baking mix such as Bisquick
1 1/2 cups milk
1 1/2 tablespoons chopped fresh parsley
1/4 cup chopped plumped sun-dried tomatoes

1. Preheat the oven to 450°F. In a large bowl, stir the baking mix, milk, parsley, and tomatoes just until a soft dough forms.

2. On a lightly floured surface, knead the dough 8 to 10 times. Roll the dough to a 1/2-inch thickness. Using a round 1 1/2-inch cookie cutter dipped in flour, cut out as many biscuits as possible; reroll the scraps and cut out as many biscuits as possible. Place the biscuits 1 inch apart on an ungreased baking sheet.

3. Bake the biscuits for 8 to 10 minutes or until they are golden brown. **Makes 18**

The Ice Cream Bombe

Ice cream and cookies, what a duo! Nothing says "special" more than this traditional concoction; feel free to use any kind of ice cream you like.

1 gallon vanilla ice cream, softened
Assorted meringue cookies
Assorted candies, for decoration
Licorice, for decoration
Candycanes, for decoration
Plastic or fabric holly leaves, for decoration

1. Spoon about 2 cups ice cream into an 8-inch mold, pressing to make sure the ice cream gets into all the crevices. Fill the mold with ice cream. With a long knife, level the top. Transfer to the freezer. Repeat with the remaining ice cream and another 8-inch mold, and freeze until both are solid.

2. To unmold, dampen a kitchen towel with hot water. Squeeze out the excess water. Remove the molds from the freezer and place the hot towel on the outside of the molds; let sit for 1 to 2 minutes. Invert 1 mold onto a plate and invert again onto a serving platter, trying not to touch the sides. Invert the second mold onto a plate and slide it onto the first mold, making sure that it is centered. Use your fingers to smooth out the seam. Return to the freezer until firm.

3. Press the meringues and candies around the center of the bombe. Wrap licorice around the top and bottom, securing with toothpicks if necessary. Gently stick the candycane into the top of the bombe. Garnish with holly leaves. Return to the freezer; before serving, let the bombe sit at room temperature for 10 minutes. **Serves 16**

Chewy Fruit Focaccia

Soft and almost cake-like, dried fruit and spices turn focaccia into a wintery dessert that can be made all year 'round!

1 package active dry yeast

1 ¼ cups warm water

1 teaspoon plus 1 tablespoon granulated sugar

3 tablespoons vegetable oil

2 large eggs

3 cups flour

½ cup dried cherries

1 cup golden raisins

½ cup honey liqueur or honey

½ to 1 cup boiling water

¼ teaspoon cinnamon

⅛ teaspoon nutmeg

2 tablespoons coarse sugar

2 tablespoons unsalted butter

¼ cup slivered almonds

1. In a small bowl, sprinkle the yeast over ¼ cup of the water. Add 1 teaspoon sugar and stir to dissolve. Let stand until foamy, about 10 minutes.

2. In the large bowl of an electric mixer at medium speed, combine the yeast mixture, the remaining water, vegetable oil, eggs, flour, and 1 tablespoon granulated sugar. With the dough hook, knead the mixture for about 7 minutes, or until smooth and silky. Generously oil a large bowl and put the dough in the bowl; turn to coat the dough. Cover with plastic wrap and let rise for 1 hour in a warm, draft-free place.

3. Meanwhile, in a small bowl, combine the cherries and raisins. Add the honey liqueur and enough boiling water to cover. Stir and let stand for 30 minutes. Drain off and discard the soaking liquid. Transfer the fruit into a paper towel–lined bowl and pat dry.

4. Turn the dough out onto a well-oiled surface and knead in the fruit until well combined. Transfer the dough to a well-oiled bowl and turn to coat. Cover the dough with plastic wrap and let rise for 30 minutes in a warm, draft-free place.

5. Meanwhile, preheat the oven to 400°F. Generously grease a baking sheet. Combine the cinnamon, nutmeg, and coarse sugar. In a small saucepan over low heat, melt the butter.

6. Turn the dough out onto the prepared baking sheet and gently pat to fill the pan. Brush the dough with melted butter; sprinkle with almonds and then the sugar mixture.

7. Bake the focaccia 20 to 25 minutes. Let cool in the pan on a wire rack 5 minutes. Cut the bread into diamond shapes about 1½ inches across. Remove the focaccia from the pan, and transfer to a wire rack to cool. **Serves 8**

Four Ways to Keep an Earlybird in the Nest

1

A good book. A really good book.

2

A sibling to giggle with.

3

A video. A quiet, compelling video.

4

A telescope to spot dawn's early light

Santa's Mochaccino Treat

Mochaccino can really be any flavor you want it to be, but plain is our favorite. If you want to walk on the wild side, go ahead and add almond, lemon, or orange extracts. For an over-the-top dessert coffee, try topping these off with softly whipped cream and cocoa powder.

Boiling water
1 cup chocolate syrup
4 cups very strong coffee or espresso, hot
2 cups milk
8 peppermint sticks, for garnish

1. Fill 8 mugs with the boiling water and let stand for 5 minutes. Discard the water.

2. In a saucepan over high heat, bring the milk just to a boil. Immediately remove the pan from the heat and transfer the milk to a blender. Leaving the top of the blender open slightly to let air escape and holding a towel over it to keep liquid from splattering, pulse the milk just until frothy.

3. Divide the chocolate syrup among the mugs; tilt to coat the insides with the syrup. Pour in the coffee or espresso and stir to combine. Top with the milk, making sure to get some froth into each cup. **Serves 8**

Frizzled Ham & Melon

Hot, salty pink ham embraces green honeydew melon for a heavenly combination worthy of your Christmas morning fete.

1 teaspoon olive oil
8 thin slices ham (prosciutto or pancetta)
8 thin wedges honeydew melon
Chives, grape tomatoes, and fresh mint springs,
   for garnish

1. In a small skillet over medium-high heat, heat a small amount of the oil. Add 2 slices of the ham and cook about 30 seconds, until golden brown. Turn the ham over and cook about 30 seconds,  until golden brown. Transfer to a paper towel–lined plate and repeat with the remaining ingredients.

2. Wrap a slice of ham around each slice of melon and transfer to a serving platter. Garnish with the chives, tomatoes, and mint sprigs. **Serves 4**

Cheddar-Mushroom Omelettes

These omelettes are a snap to whip up, making them so good on Christmas morning.

¼ cup (½ stick) unsalted butter
2 cups sliced mushrooms
10 large eggs
¼ cup milk
Salt and freshly ground black pepper, to taste
1 cup shredded Cheddar cheese
Grape tomatoes and fresh parsley, for garnish

1. In a skillet over medium heat, melt 2 tablespoons of butter. Add the mushrooms and cook until soft. Remove from heat and set aside.

2. In a bowl, whisk together the eggs and milk; season with salt and pepper. In a large skillet over medium-high heat, melt the remaining 2 tablespoons butter. Pour the egg mixture into the skillet. Let the mixture set 1 minute. Then, using a heatproof rubber spatula, pull the eggs from the edges of the pan toward the center, tilting the pan so the excess uncooked egg comes in contact with the pan. Continue around the pan until no uncooked egg remains.

3. Pour the mushrooms over the eggs and then sprinkle with the cheese. Turn the heat off, cover, and cook 2 minutes, or until the cheese has melted. Slide the egg mixture onto waxed paper, top side up, and roll like a burrito. Transfer to large platter and serve immediately. **Serves 4**

Raspberry-White Chocolate Muffins

Sweet white chocolate and red raspberries mix with oats to form these wonderful muffins that will wake up even the sleepiest elf.

1 ½ cups quick rolled oats
1 cup flour
½ cup sugar
1 tablespoon baking powder
½ teaspoon salt
1 cup milk
2 large eggs, lightly beaten
2 tablespoons melted butter
1 teaspoon vanilla
¾ cup fresh or frozen raspberries
½ cup white chocolate chunks

1. Heat the oven to 400°F. Line 12 muffin cups with paper liners.

2. In a bowl, combine the oats, flour, sugar, baking powder and salt and mix well. In a small bowl, combine the milk, eggs, melted butter, and vanilla and mix well.

3. Add the milk mixture to the dry mixture and stir just until combined. Gently stir in the raspberries and white chocolate. Fill the prepared muffin cups two-thirds full.

4. Bake the muffins 20 to 25 minutes, or until a toothpick inserted in the center comes out clean. Cool the muffins in the pan on a wire rack for 5 minutes. Remove from the pan and serve. **Makes 1 dozen**

Cherry, Cream, Marshmallow & Walnut Parfaits

Sweet red gelatin layered with fluffy whipped cream and topped with nuts, what a celestial trio!

Two 3 ounces cherry-flavored gelatin
2 cups boiling water
2 cups cold water
¾ cup halved and pitted fresh cherries or other berries
3 tablespoons chopped walnuts, plus additional for garnish
½ cup mini marshmallows
1 12-ounce container whipped topping
Coarse red sugar, for garnish

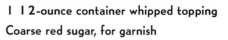

1. In a bowl, whisk together the gelatin and boiling water until it is smooth. Gently stir in the cold water until combined. Cover with plastic wrap and refrigerate about 1 to 1½ hours, until the gelatin is slightly thickened. Fold in the cherries, nuts, and marshmallows. Cover with plastic wrap and let set for at least 2 hours.

2. Layer the gelatin and whipped topping in stemmed glasses, beginning and ending with the gelatin. Top with a dollop of whipped topping and sprinkle with the additional nuts and a pinch of red sugar. **Serves 4**

workshop

W ho hasn't experienced a charge of excitement browsing through the fabric shop, the crafts store, and the holiday decorating section? Most of us have thought, too, that the decoration or gift in a photo would be more appropriate for us if the ribbon was different or the colors changed. These crafts are designed to be personalized. We urge you to substitute, eliminate, add on—to make these your very own.

Holiday Workbench

Most of the decorations and presents in this book are quick and easy to make, with no need for high-tech shop tools. A couple projects involve computer work but that can be substituted with handmade materials; we do that at the Studio all the time! Another good tip from our crafters is to have more than one pair of scissors, tape and dispenser, craft knife, and glue gun (whatever you need most often, others in the family will too!).

The Usual Supplies

Glue gun and glue sticks

White glue

Sobo glue

Spray adhesive

Fun Tac

Pushpins

Picture hangers

Gesso

Sealant

Small paintbrushes

Floral and hanging wire

Sewing machine

Assorted needles and thread

Tape measure and ruler

Scissors and craft knife

Iron

Handy Stuff

Spray snow

Pinking sheers

Double-stick tape

Gold and silver paint markers

Kraft paper

Foil curlicues

Copper wire

Ribbons and fabrics

Miniature ornaments

Holiday stickers

Cinnamon sticks

Assorted beads

Glitter

Jingle bells

Excelsior, Oh Excelsior!

Excelsior, those slender crinkled pieces of paper, comes in so handy for the holidays.

1. Pretty protective padding for cookies, candies, pies and cakes.

2. Frilly filler for stockings, paper cones, and gift baskets.

3. Amusing change from tissue paper. Gift box lining.

A Square Wreath

Break away from the ordinary round wreath! Square, diamond, teardrop, or heart are interesting options. To save time, order green wreaths preshaped, then do the fun part—the decorating!

- Green floral wire
- Square wreath form
- Fresh greens, including spruce, juniper, cyprus, and pine
- Variety of ornaments, including toys, puppets, cinnamon sticks, faux fruit, foil curlicues, and raffia
- Polka-dot ribbon

1. Wrap the floral wire around the top center of the wreath form, adding more wire for a hanging loop. Knot the wire around itself to secure.

2. Wind the floral wire at the stems of the greenery and wire the greens to the wreath form. Make sure to cover both the top and the sides of the form with the greens. Preheat a glue gun.

3. Cluster ornaments into bunches of 4 to 6. Use the glue gun to glue them together. Let dry for 5 minutes. Glue the clusters to the wreath. Use floral wire to secure heavier items to the wreath.

4. Tie the ribbon into a big bow. Glue the ribbon to the top center of the wreath. Let dry for 5 minutes.

Holly & Gingham Door Greeting

Slim and chirpy, this door embellishment sends a unique welcome.

- Window Stencils, pages 136-137
- Stencil paper or clear plastic that can be used in a photocopier
- Beveled-edge mirrors
- Spray snow
- Strip of sturdy cardboard
- Gingham ribbon
- Variegated holly leaves

1. Photocopy the patterns to the desired size onto the stencil paper. Use a craft knife to cut out the designs.

2. On a covered work surface, position a stencil on 1 mirror. Wearing rubber gloves, lightly mist the mirror with spray snow. Let dry completely. Carefully remove the stencil, lifting it straight up. Allow the stencils to dry completely between applications. Repeat to complete the mirrors.

3. To make the hanging loop, punch a large hole in the cardboard strip, centered about 1" from the top edge. Cut a piece of ribbon, thread it through the hole, and tie into a knot, making a loop. Preheat a glue gun.

4. Starting just under the ribbon loop, glue the mirrors to the cardboard strip, gluing all the way around and leaving about 1" between each mirror. Let dry completely. Trim any excess cardboard at the bottom.

5. Cut 3 even pieces of ribbon. Tie bows around the cardboard in-between the mirrors, covering the cardboard. Glue the ribbon into place. Add the holly leaves around the bows, poking the stems into the bow knots and behind the mirrors. If necessary, glue into place.

Grandma's Stencil Windows

Quick and easy and inexpensive! Bear in mind that window stencil designs are best when they can be "read" from both sides. Don't forget to use these on your mirrors inside.

- Window Stencils, pages 136-137
- Stencil paper or clear plastic that can be used in a photocopier
- Spray snow or Glass-Wax window cleaner

1. Photocopy the patterns to the desired size onto the stencil paper. To write a message, draw letters freehand. Use a craft knife to cut out the designs and letters.

2. Position a stencil on the window and tape the corners to the glass to secure (be sure it can be read from side desired). Wearing rubber gloves, lightly mist the mirror with spray snow. Let the snow dry completely. Carefully lift the stencil straight up and remove. For Glass Wax, moisten a sponge in the product, then daub on the window to fill in the stencil. The stencils can be reused; allow them to dry completely between applications.

Wrapsody in Giving

Do you draw up a holiday shopping budget, spend carefully to meet it, then freak out over the cost of papers and ribbons when you're ready to wrap? Here's help.

Hand-painted paper sacks are such practical gift wrap: they are cheerful, sturdy, accommodate myriad shapes, and don't even need cello tape. Plus they're strong enough to be used over and over.

These are painted with a variety of images in non-washable paints. Some designs are stencils, others freehand. Once the paint is dry and the present has been slipped in, a short piece of ribbon is tied into a bow, just for tradition. The recipient's name can be painted on the bag or a gift tag can be attached to the ribbon.

Birdland USA

Fun for all ages! Cover the dining room table with newspaper and let everyone get to work. These sweet houses make terrific presents, too. Prop the village with miniature street lamps, mailboxes, bottlebrush trees, cotton ball tufts of snow, and a circular mirror to serve as a skating pond. Or get a little goofy with palm trees, flamingos, and surfboards.

FOR HOUSES
- Unfinished wood or cardboard birdhouses
- Gesso
- Acrylic craft paint
- "Snow" paint
- Clear glitter

FOR STOCKINGS
- Card stock
- Felt
- Colored glitter
- Ribbon
- Miniature wreaths, birds, and other props

1. Paint the exterior of the birdhouse with an even, thin coat of gesso. Allow the gesso to dry completely.

2. Use the craft paint to paint the roofs one color and the houses a second color. Let dry completely, and apply a second coat if needed. Add some painted accents around the entrance or at the base, if desired. Apply "snow" paint to the roof, letting the heavy paint drip down in a natural way. Sprinkle the wet paint with clear glitter.

3. To make the stockings, draw stocking shapes on the card stock. Use a craft knife to cut the shapes out. Cut cuffs out of the felt to fit the stocking tops; trim one long edge with a wavy top. Paint the stockings with a thin coat of white glue, sprinkle on colored glitter. Glue on the cuffs. Let the stockings dry.

4. Preheat a glue gun. Using the glue gun, glue a bit of folded ribbon to the back of the top corner of the stockings. Let cool completely. Glue the ribbons to the edges of the birdhouses. Glue on wreaths, birds, and other ornaments. Let the birdhouses dry completely.

5. Arrange the birdhouses and other elements on shelves, a mantel, a piano, a hall table, of wherever you like. Add street signs, shop signs, telephone poles and wires, trees, and other accessories.

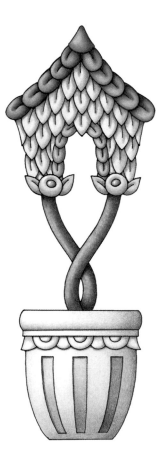

Candle Glow but Safe

If you love the soft look of candlelight but fret about fire safety, consider the string of fairy lights. Like candles, it casts a gentle glow but without the open flame. From mantel to tabletop, fairy lights bring a twinkle to any scene.

Advent Wall Quilt

An heirloom, to be sure, our wall quilt can be grand or petit. If you'd like one just for your family, replace the numbers on the pockets with everyone's initials. Tuck on pockets for future generations.

- Templates, pages 138-139
- Felt
- Assorted fabric for the pockets and strips
- 26 pairs Velcro dots
- 26 buttons
- Red, white, and green felt for the numerals

1. Calculate the dimensions of the finished wall quilt using the template as a guide. Cut a piece of felt to the finished size. Cut the fabric into strips to be placed horizontally and vertically to form the grid, following the template.

2. Turn the long edges of all the strips under ¼" on each side and press with an iron. Position the fabric on the felt following the template. Pin to secure and sew.

3. Measure and cut 4 fabric pieces for frame, following the template. Turn the edges under ¼" and press. Pin, overlapping the vertical and horizontal pieces, and sew.

4. To make the pockets, cut 24 pockets from fabric, following the template.

5. For each pocket, turn the edges under ¼" and press. Following the template, fold the 2 top corners of the rectangle toward the center of the wrong side of the fabric to form a point. Baste the corners together where they meet. Fold the bottom of the rectangle up to meet the flap. Fold the flap over. Press.

6. Sew buttons to the pocket flaps at their points. Add Velcro tabs to the pockets, one just under the flap point and its mate at the top of the pocket. Cut numbers from colored felt and glue on to each pocket.

7. Pin each of the 24 pockets in position on the felt and sew close to the pocket edge along the sides and bottom.

8. To make the number 1 pocket: double the template in width. Cut, pin, and sew a larger rectangular pocket that will cover the 2 top center spaces and press.

9. To make the side triangle pockets, cut a square of fabric. Fold the fabric in half diagonally to form a triangle and press. Turn under the side and bottom edges ¼" and press. Cut 2 strips of contrasting fabric to serve as edges for the triangles. Turn the strips under ¼" on each edge to fit and press. Pin the strips to the folded edge of the triangle and sew into position. Position the triangle pockets following the template and sew.

10. For the bottom panel, cut out a piece of fabric the width of your wall quilt. With right sides facing and edges aligned, stitch it to the bottom of the felt backing. Turn and press.

11. Cut fabric into 5 strips to cover the edges of the wall quilt and the seam of the bottom panel. Turn the edges under ¼" on the long sides and press.

12. Pin the edging fabric in position, folding it over the sides and bottom of the wall quilt. Sew into position. Press.

13. For hangers, cut 5 fabric strips as indicated on the template. With right sides facing, sew a ¼" seam down the long edge of each strip. Turn right side out and press.

14. Sew the tabs to the back of the top edge of the hanging, short edges meeting in back. Hang the quilt by the loops from a rod.

The Holiday Tote

You'll never face Christmas with dismay again once you've created this eye-catching, incredibly useful tote. The artwork on the front actually conceals a roomy pocket.

- Let It Snow artwork for transfer, page 140*
- 8 ½" x 6" white fabric
- 7" x 9 ½" patterned fabric
- Large canvas tote bag
- Fringe
- Guimpe or trim

1. At the copyshop, have the artwork copied for transfer to fabric. Iron the image onto the white fabric. Turn the edges of the fabric under by ¼" and  iron. Center the image on the patterned fabric. Pin and sew around the edges of the image. Turn the edges of the patterned fabric under by ¼" and iron.

2. Stitch the bottom and 2 short sides of the pocket to the tote bag. Center this piece onto the side of the tote.

3. Sew or hot-glue the fringe, then the trim around the top of the bag. If you like, stitch some jingle bells around the fringe.

Even Better: If you like, line the tote bag. A light color fabric can help you to see inside the bag, especially if you've chosen a deep color canvas. Sew the front and back panels of lining together and stitch the lining to the top of the tote bag before adding the trims. Pull the lining out, fold the open end under ¼", and sew the edges together. Insert the lining into the tote.

*Copying of this image is permitted for personal use only, and the image may not be reproduced in quantity. All other rights reserved.

Ornament Treasure Boxes

What did we ever do without these? Make them for your ornaments, or to give as a gift, filled with vintage finds.

- Toile fabric
- Square cardboard box with lid
- Ribbon
- Ornaments, heirlooms, and trinkets

1. Turn the box upside down. Lay the fabric over to position the design best on the sides. Hold the fabric in place on the box and turn right side up. Lay  the fabric flat again, keeping it in position. Use a pencil to mark the outline of the box bottom on the wrong side of the fabric. Measure the box sides and extend lines out from the box this length plus 1" on the sides and ends for overlap. The pattern should look like a cross.

2. Cut the fabric according to the pattern. Turn the edges under ½" and press. Place the box bottom in the center of the fabric. With a pencil, mark the fabric around the bottom of the box.

3. In a well-ventilated work area, mist the exterior of the box with spray adhesive. Try not to get any glue inside of the box. Place the box bottom on the marked fabric and press down to secure; rub the fabric to smooth out.

4. Glue the side panels. Begin with 1 side, smoothing the fabric up the box sides and over the top by about 1". As you overlap the sides, fold the adjacent sides to make a straight seam at the box-side edges.

5. Brush white glue under the overlapping fabric strips and press on the inside of the box-side to secure.

6. Repeat the measuring, cutting, and gluing process with the box lid. Preheat a glue gun.

7. Glue 2 strips of ribbon to the box bottom and opposite sides, overlapping the top edges by about an inch. With the glue gun, secure the ribbon overlap to the inside of the box. Repeat for the box lid, matching the ribbon placement on the box bottom.

8. Tie 4 ribbon bows and glue them to the ribbons on the box lid on the front and back. Trim the bows' edges to match. Let dry completely.

9. Fill the boxes with your choice of favorite ornaments, heirlooms, and trinkets from Christmases past.

Holiday Cheer Wallhanging

Make your favorite greeting card a banner for your dinner buffet.

- **Pattern, page 141 or holiday card**
- **Foamcore**
- **Self-adhesive picture hanger**
- **Greenery**
- **Garlands**
- **Fairy lights**

1. At the copyshop, have the artwork color copied to the desired size.

2. Using spray adhesive, mount the printout on foamcore. Let dry completely.

3. Center and attach the picture hanger on the foamcore and hang it on the wall. Surround the hanging with sprigs of pine, garlands, and fairy lights, securing each with removable adhesive hangers.

Live, Love, Laugh & Be Happy

Crafters will eagerly tell you that the joy is in the making. Handmade stuff, whether it's just for the day or a gift for a lifetime, is such a personal expression. Perfection isn't the goal for the majority; it's often the little goof that is the most endearing part of a piece.

Greetings under Glass

Keep your favorite holiday cards preserved for Christmases to come. Each year set aside the cards that inspired you and then frame them for next year.

- Christmas cards
- Sheets of glass with polished edges
- Rickrack
- Tinsel or braid
- Small ornaments

1. Trim the front of the Christmas card to the size and shape desired. Measure the card. Have a glass store cut a piece of glass to the desired sizes and polish the edges.

2. Apply decoupage adhesive evenly to the back sides of the glass. Press the front of the card onto it, smoothing out any air bubbles or creases. Let dry completely. Preheat a glue gun.

3. Using the glue gun, glue rickrack around the edge of the front of the glass, tucking the edges over to the back.

4. Cut the tinsel or braid 2½ times as long as the desired length for hanging. On the back of the card, position each end of the tinsel about ½" from the top edge, not too close to the sides, and glue in place. Let dry completely. If desired, choose and glue on some decorative ornaments.

Greetings Galore

Combine all those fabulous framed cards into a piece that can be hung from the banister, the cupboards, or the shelves.

- 1 dozen or so Greetings under Glass, opposite
- Tinsel or braid
- Small ornaments

1. Sort the cards by theme, color, or however you wish. Cluster several cards in each group.

2. Hang each cluster of cards from a shelf or ledge, and other cards separately. Once they are hung, embellish the cards with jingle bells, star foil tinsel, and tiny glass ornaments.

Holiday-ized CD and Case

At Christmas, stores are stuffed with holiday music CDs. Jazz them up with customized sets of liner notes complete with artwork, to give as gifts or favors.

- **CD with case**
- **8½" x 11" paper**
- **Photos and images**
- **Holiday stickers**
- **CD label kit**

1. Trace the booklet from the interior of the CD onto white or colored paper, making sure the booklet is open (about 9½" x 4¾"). Cut out the shape and repeat with one more page. Fold the pages in half crosswise and insert them into the case to confirm the fit.

2. Glue or print images and a greeting to the front of the booklet. Similarly, fill the interior of the booklet with pictures, a listing of the songs, and holiday stickers. If desired, staple the booklet down the spine. Slide the booklet into the case.

3. To create a CD label, follow the manufacturer's directions for designing and printing with artwork that coordinates with the booklet for the case.

CD Greeting Card At a stationery or an office supply store, you can purchase CD templates for the computer and labels that can be fed through your printer. Choose a theme and gather images from vintage holiday cards, wrapping papers, old family photos, or other sources.

Holiday Tunes

A rainy afternoon in late November offers a good opportunity to pull together the family's holiday music. Sort through the various CDs in your library, not only for Christmas ones but also for music you find meaningful, like gospel singers, instrumentalists, choirs, jazz groups, and symphony orchestras. Organize the music by type of event you plan and avoid all that last-minute rush to the sound system.

Holiday Frames

The humble snapshot has a place in your holiday, once it's dressed up. A seasonal frame, polka-dot paper matting, and the old holiday lifesaver rickrack trim will make photos from a summer reunion perfect for a snowy celebration. For your frames, choose a bright seasonal color. Glue rhinestones around the exterior of the frame for added eye appeal. Make several, in similar frames, and turn the front entrance into a little photo gallery.

Select the photos you wish to display. Edge each picture with rickrack, securing it with a glue stick; let dry completely. Place the photo, centered, on a graphic background. Center the background in a mat or surround, place in a frame, and secure the backing.

Santa Dinnerware

Santa will be glad to put up his feet for a refreshing beverage and a cookie break when he sees this set-up. Make room for the presents!

- **Plain white china plate and cup**
- **Ceramic paints safe for food contact**
- **Small paintbrushes**

1. In your best penmanship, write a message on the plate and cup. We've used "Santa Stop Here," but you may not want to be so bossy. Feel free to let your imagination take hold! Following the manufacturer's directions, paint the lettering with ceramic paints and brushes.

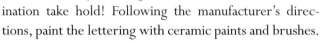
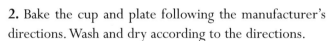

2. Bake the cup and plate following the manufacturer's directions. Wash and dry according to the directions.

3. Set the dishes in a prominent place, near a comfortable chair (encourage Santa to linger at your house). Place the best-looking, best-tasting cookie you can find upon the plate and fill the mug.

4. Cross your fingers and tiptoe to bed.

kids can do it!

Santa, Stop Here!

I Was Good for Goodness' Sake

Never Naughty; **Always Nice**

Santa, Sit Down; **Take a Load Off**

Night-before-Christmas Light

How comforting these adorable night lights are. This is the kind of project that becomes easier and faster to make in quantity, so you might consider an assembly line. They are perfect gifts for everyone!

- Night-light with shade
- White cardstock
- Holiday images
- Small snowflakes, holly stickers, or other adhesive decorations
- Cotton ball fringe
- Velcro dots

1. Remove the shade from the night-light. Trace the shade onto cardstock and cut out the shape.

2. On a covered surface, in a well-ventilated area (preferably outdoors), use spray adhesive to attach the holiday images to the paper pattern, smoothing out any bumps. Paste on other decorations as desired. Glue the fringe to the bottom edge of the paper pattern.

3. Attach the Velcro dots to the top and bottom corners of the shade and the paper pattern. Stick the paper pattern to the shade and attach to the night light.

Night-light on Duty:

We've designed the shades so they can be changed when Christmas is over. They'd be sweet with hearts for Valentine's Day, flowers in the spring, or with a name on them for someone's visit or birthday.

Say It with Feeling

Computers are terrific tools and timesavers during the holidays but, honestly, nothing from a computer can replace words written with the human hand. You protest that your penmanship is atrocious and that no one will be able to read it? Try some of these techniques and see if this doesn't become your "handheld" holiday.

1 **Develop your style.** Whether you print or prefer script, create a distinctive look for your letters and numerals.

2 **Practice.** Work with different kinds of markers, paints and brushes, crayons and chalks, to find which is most comfortable for you.

3 **Trace.** When you are challenged by an important job like painting a message on a prominent mirror, write it out first, then, when you are satisfied, trace it onto paper that can be cut into patterns. Outline the patterns in position and fill in the letters.

4 **Know what you want to say.** It is about the message, after all. A gift tag especially is cherishable when it carries meaningful thoughts.

5 **Choose** only removable inks and paints. You knew that!

Joy Bumper

"If you're close enough to read this, feel joyful" might be the bumper sticker alongside this chirpy message. This greeting is a bit of showmanship, created more for an event than everyday errands.

- Heavy wire, such as bailing wire or heavy-gauge galvanized wire
- Artificial green garland
- Floral wire
- White or ivory matte spray paint
- Battery-powered Christmas lights, with white wire
- Variety of sturdy, nonbreakable, waterproof toys, ornaments or other findings

1. Use heavy wire to form each letter. Wrap the letter in one additional length of wire for strength.

2. Wrap 1 wire letter with the garland, intermittently securing the garland to the wire with short lengths of floral wire, fluffing the garland to cover the floral wire. Repeat with the remaining letters.

3. Working on a covered surface in a well-ventilated area (preferably outdoors), lightly spray paint each letter. Let dry completely.

4. Preheat the glue gun. Wrap the lights around each letter, securing with floral wire. Using the glue guns, glue the toys and ornaments to the letters.

5. With heavy wire, secure the letters to your vehicle, taking care not to obscure the license plate or the lights.

Christmas Princess Crowns

Nothing makes it more official than a crown. Every honored guest deserves her own personal tiara.

- Plain crowns
- Assorted strings of beads
- Ribbons
- Assorted loose jewels

1. Preheat the glue gun.

2. Using the glue gun, glue the strings of beads to the crowns, allowing the beads to swag. Let dry completely. Glue the ribbons to the crowns in the same manner.

3. Glue the jewels to the crowns, covering the bead strings and ribbon ends where possible. Let dry completely.

A local costume shop should have a good selection of crowns and tiaras. If you've got lads rather than lasses, you may want to replace the jewels with feathers and choose a tartan ribbon.

Christmas Cones

We love holiday cones. They bring life to any area, even one that's already busy. Hang them across the mantel, from window shades or, as we did here, from the light fixture over the kitchen table.

- Vintage holiday images
- 8½" x 11" heavyweight paper
- Large paper clips
- Trims, fringes, and tinsel
- Ribbon
- Pom-poms
- Jingle bells

1. Photocopy or scan images and print each onto 8½" x 11" paper. Preheat a glue gun.

2. Lay the paper face down on a flat surface. Holding 1 corner, which will be the point of the cone, roll the adjacent corner toward the center. As the cone forms, tighten the twist toward the bottom point and loosen the twist at the top. Use a paper clip to hold the twist of the cone in place, then glue along the seam just under the edge. Hold the cone shape for 1 minute to dry.

3. Trim the top of the cone straight across. Punch 1 hole in the thickest part of the cone about 1" from the top and 1 hole on the opposite side about 1" from the top. Fold the ribbon in half lengthwise, thread the end through the hole toward the inside, and knot on the inside several times to secure; repeat with the second hole.

4. Glue trim, fringe, or tinsel to the top of the cone. Glue a pom-pom to the point of the cone. Drop 1 or 2 jingle bells in the bottom of each cone before filling.

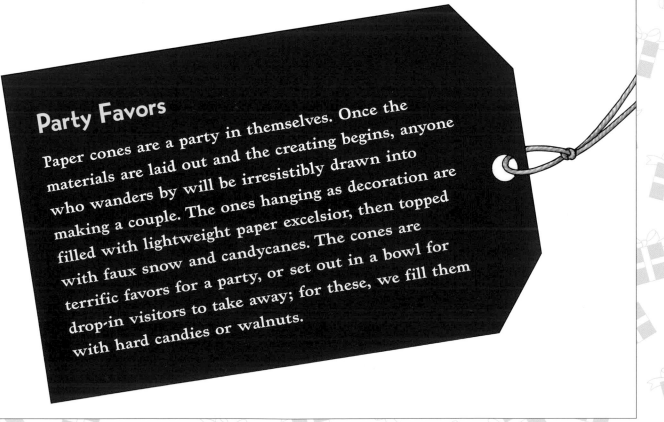

Party Favors

Paper cones are a party in themselves. Once the materials are laid out and the creating begins, anyone who wanders by will be irresistibly drawn into making a couple. The ones hanging as decoration are filled with lightweight paper excelsior, then topped with faux snow and candycanes. The cones are terrific favors for a party, or set out in a bowl for drop-in visitors to take away; for these, we fill them with hard candies or walnuts.

No-Hassle Tassel Curtain

You can create quick holiday curtains without setting up the sewing machine. These are modeled on old-fashioned window shades.

- 1 tension rod the width of the window
- Fabric the width of the window
- 1"-wide ribbon
- White cotton duck cloth
- Rickrack
- Tassel
- Scottie or other appliqué

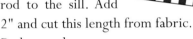

1. Position the tension rod within the window frame. Measure the distance from the rod to the sill. Add 2" and cut this length from fabric. Preheat a glue gun.

2. Glue ribbon to the sides and bottom edges of the fabric, folding and gluing at the corners.

3. Bring the top of the curtain over the tension rod from the back toward the front, with the front facing out. Aligning the bottom of the curtain with the sill, adjust the fabric folding over the rod to form a seam. Glue the seam closed.

4. Cut a triangle of cotton duck the width of the curtain and as long as you like. Glue ribbon to the long edges of the triangle. Glue rickrack to the center of the ribbon. Glue the tassel string to the back of the point.

5. Glue the appliqué to the front of the triangle. Turn the curtain face down. Position the triangle at the top of the curtain back, with the point facing up and the appliqué facing you. Glue the triangle edge to the top of the curtain. Flip the triangle over the tension rod and hang the curtain.

Stitches in Time

The mighty computer can't replace painstaking hand embroidery, but sometimes it can improve on it! These don't have the sentiment of authenticity, but they look fabulous!

Have the imagery scanned and enlarged or reduced to size. Transfer the scan to a computer disk. Take the fabric and disk to a sewing center or quilt shop for output. Adapt this idea for tablecloths, placemats and napkins, pillow cases, and even family banners. Consider new fabric or vintage pieces; the one below is actually a soft, downy flour sack. Another neat idea is to paste the greeting onto paper and turn it into a greeting card; it's the same, only better!

Take Me to Candyland!

Please don't eat the trees! Candyland is designed to gaze upon, to scrutinize, to adore, but not to eat. It's a fantasy, but one that will set off the candy alarm in every visitor. Our advice? Station bowls of candy for guests' consumption everywhere around the room.

Gumdrop Topiary

Any kind of hard candy will do here, just make sure it is bright and colorful!

- Terra-cotta pot
- Snow paint
- Styrofoam filler
- 2 large white paper lollipop sticks
- 1 large and 1 small Styrofoam ball
- Gumdrops for lower ball
- Hard candies for top ball

1. With the snow paint, decorate the top of the terra-cotta pot to simulate a collar of snow. Allow to dry completely. Fill the pot with Styrofoam and set aside. Preheat a glue gun.

2. Insert a lollipop stick in each Styrofoam ball. Using the glue gun, glue the candies around the surface of both balls. Allow to dry completely.

3. Insert the stick of the larger ball into the foam-filled pot. Insert the stick of the smaller ball in-between the candies on the larger ball. Cover the foambase in the pot with sourballs.

Licorice Garland for Tree

Scotties on the tree? You bet! These little pups will be barking across the branches all season long.

- Clear nylon thread
- Upholstery needle
- Licorice Scotties
- Sugar-candy pieces
- Gumballs

1. Thread the needle and tie off one end. Pierce a Scottie and pull the thread through.

2. Wrap thread around a chunk of sugar candy, then thread through a gumball.

3. Continue threading around the rock sugar candy and through the soft candies, alternating each for variety. Tie off the end of the string. Drape the garland over the branches of the tree.

A Ribbon Runs Through It

Curvaceous and lustrous, ribbon candy is one of the most beloved Christmas treats. Though it's been around for generations, technology hasn't been able to make it any finer. Ribbon candy is so much fun peeking out of a stocking top, as the ribbon on a gift, and as part of a tabletop decoration. You can't have too much ribbon candy on hand for the holidays.

Pinwheel Wreath

If you've got a glue gun, you've got this snappy peppermint wreath. Don't bother to remove the cellophane from the candies; it will help to keep them in position. Hang the wreath over a mirror and you'll get double enjoyment from it.

- Styrofoam wreath base
- Cellophane-wrapped peppermints or sourballs
- Ribbon

1. Heat a glue gun. Glue a peppermint and position on the base. Repeat until the base is covered and allow to dry completely. Tie a piece of ribbon around the wreath and hang.

String of Peppermint Pearls

Peppermints signal that winter is upon us and their joyful red and white color is a lovely accent to any part of your home.

- Cellophane-wrapped peppermints
- Cellophane-wrapped candy canes

1. Heat a glue gun.

2. Decide on a pattern for the peppermints and candy canes; it could be evenly spaced or totally irregular. Arrange the candies and glue one to another.

3. Tie a length of ribbon around the peppermint at each end to secure in position.

templates

Window Stencils

Advent
Wall Quilt

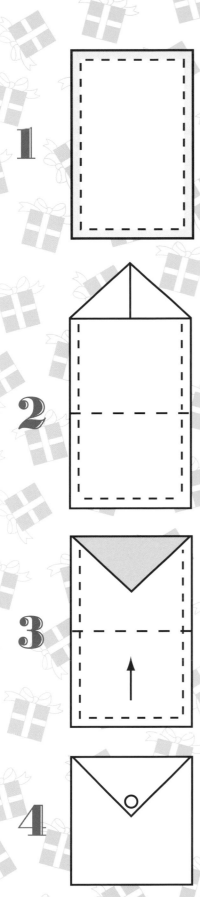

1

2

3

4

Tote Bag

Resources

It's Time for Mistletoe and Holly

PAGE 16
Spray Snow and Spray Frost available at Michaels, 800-MICHAELS, www.michaels.com

PAGE 18
Cut Glass Ornaments available at Hobby Lobby, hobbylobby.com

PAGE 19
Individual Unfinished Birdhouses, Acrylic Paint, and Snow Paint available at Michaels, 800-MICHAELS, www.michaels.com

PAGE 26
Assorted Christmas Fabric available at The Quilt Store, Austin, TX 512-453-1145

PAGE 29
Assorted Toys in Fabric Wall hanging available at Cost Plus World Market, www.costplus.com

PAGE 30
Round Metal-Rimmed Tags available at Office Depot, 888-GO-DEPOT, www.officedepot.com
Assorted Christmas Buttons available at Hancock Fabrics, www.hancockfabrics.com

PAGE 38
Plain Red Tote available at Michaels, 800-MICHAELS, www.michaels.com
Looped Ribbon Fringe and **Red Guimpe,** Gelberg Braid. Call 212-730-1121 for a participating retailer near you.

The Stockings Are Hung

PAGE 45
Tin Pails available at Schylling, 800-SOS-TOYS, www.schylling.com

PAGE 46
Uncovered Papier Mâché boxes available at DC&C, 316-685-6265,
Christmas Toile available at The Quilt Store, Austin, TX 512-453-1145
Red Grosgrain Ribbon from Offray, 908-879-4700

PAGE 47
Shadowbox available at Michaels, 800-MICHAELS, www.michaels.com

PAGE 51
Martini and Champagne Glasses available at Pier1 Imports, 800-245-4595, www.pier1.com

PAGE 52
Red Dishware available at Vietri, 800-277-5933, www.vietri.com

PAGE 64
Red Bowl available at Vietri, 800-277-5933, www.vietri.com
Glass Holly Plate available at Clarksville Pottery, 512-454-9079

Joy to the World